If God Is in Control,
Why Is My Life
Such a Mess?

If God Is in Control, Why Is My Life Such a Mess?

Michael Youssef

THOMAS NELSON PUBLISHERS
Nashville

Published in Nashville, Tennessee, by Thomas Nelson, Inc.

Unless otherwise noted, Scripture quotations are from the HOLY BIBLE: NEW INTERNATIONAL VERSION. Copyright © 1973, 1978, 1984 by International Bible Society. Used by permission of Zondervan Publishing House. All rights reserved.

Scripture quotations noted KJV are from the KING JAMES VERSION of the Holy Bible.

Library of Congress Cataloging-in-Publication Data

Youssef, Michael.
     If God is in control, why is my life such a mess? / Michael
Youssef.
          p. cm.
     Includes bibliographical references.
     ISBN 0-7852-7103-1 (pbk.)
     1. Providence and government of God. 2. Elijah (Biblical
prophet) 3. Esther, Queen of Persia. I. Title.
BT135.Y85 1998
248.8'6—dc21
                                        98–35499
                                            CIP

Printed in the United States of America
1 2 3 4 5 6 QPK 03 02 01 00 99 98

*To my wife and best friend, Elizabeth, who often
reminds me of how sovereign God really is!*

Contents

Contents

Acknowledgments

It is with heartfelt gratitude that I make the following acknowledgments to a number of people who helped make this book a reality.

I thank Connie Reece for her editorial skills, never trying to change my words but enhance them. Connie worked tirelessly to blend my own life story with that of Elijah's without forgetting that Elijah was the prophet of God and not I. I also thank Janet Thoma at Thomas Nelson Publishers for her persistence in challenging me to open my heart and life to my readers.

I express my thanks to Brenda Williams for handling the many details that go into finalizing a book.

Ultimately, I am thankful to the faithful members of The Church of The Apostles in Atlanta, Georgia, who, when they heard this series of messages, urged me to put them into print.

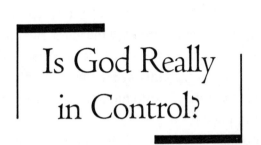

one

Is God Really in Control?

I entered the Ministry of War Department with the words of my friends ringing in my ears.

"They'll never give you an exit visa," one of them had told me. "You could end up in the army before you leave the building."

"Or in jail!" another friend added.

Pushing their warnings out of my mind, I stepped through the door. My footsteps echoed on the tile floor as I walked toward the receptionist. *God, You are calling me out of Egypt,* I prayed silently. *That means I need an exit visa, so here I am. You will have to provide a way for me to leave.*

I tried to sound more confident than I felt. "Which official is in charge of granting exit visas?"

The man sitting behind the desk looked at me skeptically but provided me with the name of a particular general.

"Where is his office?"

"You're wasting your time," the receptionist said. But when I insisted, he pointed me in the right direction.

When I found the minister's outer office, I explained to his secretary what I wanted. "It will only take a few minutes," I told him. "I really need to see the general in person."

"You may not see him," he said. "And even if you did, you would not get your visa approved."

"Why don't you let me go in and find out for myself?"

"You're a university student, aren't you?" he asked. I nodded. "No visas for university students."

"But I have—"

"No exceptions."

I tried every argument I could think of, but nothing worked. Finally, knowing I was defeated, I left. The situation was out of my control.

But I still had my "marching orders" from the Lord: He had called me to preach, and He had directed me to leave Egypt. So the next day I was back at the Ministry of War Department, going through the same procedure with the general's secretary. Same result: "No visas, no exceptions."

Day after day I returned, only to be turned away.

After several weeks of being refused, I spent an entire night in prayer. Very early the next morning, on a Sunday, I showed up at the minister's office.

One of the guards saw me approach the secretary. He listened to our interchange for a while and then walked over to the desk. "What is the trouble?" the guard asked.

"The general will not grant visas to any university student." The secretary nodded at me and glared. "Not for any reason."

"But I have this invitation." I showed my letter from a friend in Lebanon. "It is a request for me to visit Beirut for one week. Surely the general can allow this."

"No one gets out," the secretary argued. "It's a government regulation."

"Who does the general think he is—God?" The guard turned to me and smiled, pointing to the door. "You go in there and see the general." He stared at the secretary, defying him to object.

I thanked the guard as I hurried past the desk. Even before I reached the door, I could hear the general's voice. He was on the telephone and was using some of the foulest language I had ever heard. I knocked anyway, and without waiting for an answer, went inside.

A man wearing the uniform of an army general stood behind a massive desk in the huge office. The atmosphere was quite intimidating. I guessed the general was part of the top brass that Gamal Abdel Nasser, head of Egypt's military regime, had handpicked for this bureaucracy in order to discipline military personnel. Our troops had been decimated by Israel during the Six-Day War one year earlier; many soldiers had left the army, and morale remained low.

The general continued cursing into the telephone until he noticed me. He quickly ended the call and turned to glare at me.

"What do you want?" he growled.

I stared at him, praying for courage.

"Well, what in the [expletive] do you want?"

I stepped forward and showed him my visa application. The general grabbed it out of my hand and dropped it on the corner of his desk. "Don't you think I know why you're here? You're trying to escape national service. I know your kind." He ranted for several minutes.

Then he glanced at my application and picked it up. "Michael! Your name is Michael!" He spit out the words furiously, knowing that in a predominantly Muslim country only a Christian would have that name. "You dare to come in here when you're from the worst segment of society? You Christians are nothing but scheming traitors!"

I could not utter a word. Fear began crawling through me, and my body shook like a leaf clinging to a tree on a windy autumn day. While the general yelled, I prayed silently. *Lord, this is not the answer to prayer I was expecting. You sent me here, so please do something.*

In Conformity with God's Will

God did intervene, of course, and I was eventually granted an exit visa to leave Egypt, the country of my birth. I will finish telling the story of my personal exodus in a moment, but first I want to share the purpose for narrating these events for you.

Like the prophet Jeremiah,[1] I was called to preach while I was in my mother's womb. My mother already had six children and was in very poor health when she became pregnant with me. Because of her medical condition, the doctor recommended an abortion, and she scheduled the procedure. Just before she entered the hospital, however, our pastor made an unusual late-night visit to our house. My parents immediately knew that the purpose of his visit was quite serious.

"Noza," he said to my mother, "I have a word for you from the Lord."

"Then let us hear it," my father said.

"You are not to terminate this pregnancy," Pastor Ayad Girgis said. "I am well aware of your health problems, and I would never come to you with such advice if I did not believe with complete certainty that God had sent me."

He shared with my parents how he had been unable to sleep for several nights, and how he had sought God about their situation. They listened patiently, not quite understanding, but wanting to be obedient to God's will.

"God is involved in this pregnancy," the pastor said. "Do not be afraid. You will have the strength and health to raise this child, because this child will be born to serve the Lord."

My parents understood this message to mean that their yet-unborn child, their seventh, would grow up to be a minister of God. No one in their families had ever been a minister, and the news came as quite a surprise to them. Devout Christians, they accepted the pastor's message as God's word, and they obeyed.

Though it was a very dramatic episode in my family's life, my prenatal calling is actually not as momentous as it may sound. You see, God knows each one of us intimately, and He has a plan for our lives—a plan that He puts into effect before we are born.

The psalmist describes God's providence over our lives in this way:

> For you created my inmost being;
> > you knit me together in my mother's womb . . .
> All the days ordained for me
> > were written in your book
> > before one of them came to be. (Ps. 139:13, 16)

Before you were even born, God determined your life span—"all the days ordained" for you. That is a very comforting thought if you understand the sovereignty of God. As I write these words, this is day number 18,134 of my life. I do not know whether I will be here for day number 18,135—but God does. So why should I worry about tomorrow? He already knows what, if anything, tomorrow holds for me.

God not only knows the number of my days, He knows the number of hairs on my head. (I'm not sure I want to keep track of that number!) When the Bible says that the hairs of our head are numbered,[2] it does not mean that God has simply *counted* how many hairs are on your head. No, He has *numbered* the hairs on your head—meaning He knows exactly which ones are now in your hairbrush. God has chronological records of the strands of your hair.

Not even a sparrow falls to the earth without the heavenly Father's knowledge. He is the Creator of every living thing, and He watches over all of His creation down to the tiniest of details.

Yet when tragedies occur, or when wickedness seems to triumph, many people ask, "Where is God? Why did He let this happen?" When struggling to stay afloat on a sea of difficult circumstances, even the seasoned believer is tempted to ask, "If God is in control, why is my life such a mess?"

Let me assure you, God is in absolute control of

His creation. He governs the universe and everything that happens in it. But much of Christianity fails to recognize divine providence in daily events; we have lost the proper understanding of the sovereignty of God. We fail to see the "big picture" of God's sovereign plan for the universe.

Another misunderstanding about the biblical concept of the sovereignty of God is the fatalistic attitude that says, "If God is in complete control of events, then it doesn't matter what I do." That is quite wrong. What you do matters a great deal. God created us with the capacity for free will. We have the ability to make choices, and those choices have consequences, for good or evil. As we will see, our free will has already been factored into God's overall plan.

What the sovereignty of God really means is this: *God is in control.* He has a plan for my life, a plan for your life—and we are part of His plan for the entire universe. From the moment of creation until now, God has been working out His sovereign plan, which the apostle Paul explained in the first chapter of Ephesians:

> And he made known to us the mystery of his will according to his good pleasure, which he purposed in Christ, to be put into effect when the times will have reached their fulfillment—to bring all things in heaven and on earth together under one head, even Christ. In him we were also

chosen, having been predestined according to the plan of him who works out everything in conformity with the purpose of his will. (vv. 9–11)

One of the areas we will explore in these pages is the importance of prayer. Even though God is in control and He is working everything out in conformity with His eternal plan, He still instructs us to pray. As contradictory as it sounds, our prayers can play a vital role in changing the course of events in a particular situation. And that underscores the need for us to pray in accordance with God's will. Too many of our prayers are focused on trying to accomplish *our* plans and purposes, not the divine purposes of God. Our goal in prayer should be to determine how we can fit into and further God's sovereign plan. When we pray in this manner, God will allow us a glimpse into His eternal perspective on events—a sneak preview, if you will, of what lies just ahead of us.

With that in mind, let me finish telling the story of my exodus from Egypt. I want to show you very briefly how God led me into His divine will, how He fulfilled His plan for my life, and how He answered my prayers to that end.

"Just Pray. I Will Intervene."

As a teenager, I had surrendered to God's call on my life. Along with that inner call came a strong conviction that God had called me into a preaching ministry—but not in Egypt.

"If not Egypt, then where?" I had asked God.

"The United States," came the answer.

I did not hear the voice of God, and no further word came to me, but in my heart I knew the answer: I was to leave Egypt. God would open the door at the right time. No matter how impossible it seemed at the moment, I had a deep assurance that I would receive my training for the ministry in another country, and that I would eventually be in ministry in the United States of America.

I had no idea how God could possibly work this out. By 1968 life had become extremely difficult in Egypt, especially for Christians. Nationalism was on the rise, and contempt for the followers of Christ was growing. I detested the Nasser regime and its Socialist ideals. As soon as I finished my university studies, I would have to enroll for military service, and the country was already preparing to fight Israel again. If I stayed in Egypt, I could not refuse to serve. But how would I ever be able to leave?

I did what I had learned from my mother's example: I began to fast and pray. Almost by the hour the certainty grew that God was leading me to emigrate from Egypt. For the next several weeks I did not attend classes. Instead I used the time to make the rounds of the foreign embassies. My first choice, the American embassy, had closed after the Six-Day War. Canada, I learned, was no longer accepting immigrants. But when I visited the Australian embassy, I received good news. I filled out an application for immigration on the spot.

Subsequently, one of my brothers contacted an Australian friend who agreed to sponsor me. I had a physical exam and went through a series of interviews. And at the end of six months the embassy notified me that I had been accepted for immigration to Australia. All I had to do was get a passport and a prepaid airline ticket. I picked up my immigration papers and left the embassy rejoicing in God's answer to my prolonged prayer.

The very same day, however, Nasser issued a new ruling: No university student could hold a passport, and no university student could travel abroad. With my permission to immigrate to Australia, I should have been out of the country in a matter of days; now I was trapped. Under the new rules there would be no leaving Egypt.

What do you suppose I asked God? If you answered "why," you are exactly right. "How could You allow this to happen?" I asked. "Why didn't You delay Nasser's ruling by just a day or two?" The situation did not make sense, but I had to trust that God was in control of the situation.

As I continued to seek God, two sentences kept coming into my mind. "Just pray. I will intervene." So I continued to pray. What other option did I have?

After many weeks I received a letter from a university friend who had returned to his home in Beirut. He had promised to send me an invitation to visit, knowing I would use the opportunity to try to leave Egypt permanently. If people in my country wanted to visit another Arab country[3] for a week or less, they would be considered for an exit visa. If I could get an exit visa, I could then apply for a passport—something I would need if I ever hoped to immigrate to Australia or anywhere else.

To get the visa required a visit to the Ministry of War Department. And that's how I wound up in the general's office, listening to his tirade against Christians.

Who Is in Control?

"I know how to fix you!" he yelled at me. "I know what to do with Christians and other traitors. I will put you in a place where no one will ever find you again. You cannot run away from your duty to your country. Don't think I won't make an example—"

In the middle of this bombastic outburst, another general entered the office. He did not acknowledge me but marched quickly to the desk, cutting off the minister in midsentence. A problem had arisen with a particular officer, and the two generals began to discuss it as if I were not even in the room.

In their heated discussion they seemed to have forgotten about me. The sensible thing to do, I decided, would be to slip out of the office while I had the chance. Having been threatened with jail, I did not want to provoke the general any further.

Cautiously I took a step backward. Then another. About to turn around and walk all the way to the door, I caught the visitor looking my way. "What does this young man want?" he asked.

"An exit visa to visit Lebanon. Stupid boy!"

"Oh, just let him go," the second general said. While the minister in charge protested, the visiting general reached for my visa application, which was still on the desk. "Here, son." He took the application, signed and stamped it with the official ministry seal, and handed it back to me. "Now, go. Get out of here."

I could not leave fast enough! On my way out I flashed my visa approval at the secretary and waved at the guard who had let me in the general's office— but I did not slow down. Once outside, I crossed the street and sat down on a park bench. My body was still shaking, and I was so queasy I almost vomited. I stared at the paper in my hand. The signature and the stamp were there. God had done the impossible.

I'd better pull myself together, I thought. I hurried to the passport office, where I submitted my exit visa and received clearance for a passport, which I would have to pay for and pick up the next day.

When I returned the following day, the officer who issued my passport said, "You must leave Egypt within forty-eight hours from the time your visa was issued. If you do not, the passport and exit visa are automatically revoked."

How could I get ready to leave overnight? I had thought it would take weeks; now I learned I had to fly out the next day or my chance to leave Egypt would evaporate, possibly forever.

With my passport in hand, I went to the office of Egypt Airlines to book my ticket. The agent shook her head. "I am sorry. That is impossible. All flights are booked for the next six days."

"But I can't wait that long." I showed her my passport and exit visa. "I have to leave by tomorrow."

"This is a religious holiday period," she said, referring to an Islamic holiday. She obviously did not intend to do anything to help a Christian.

"But I only need one seat."

"Yes, of course, but hundreds of others are ahead of you. They also wish only one seat. And some of them have been waiting for weeks for a cancellation."

Dejected and perplexed, I left the ticket office. *Okay, God,* I prayed silently as I walked, *what do I do now?* Immediately I thought of a Christian friend who worked for Egypt Airlines, so I headed for his office.

He confirmed what the ticket agent had said. "Michael, here is the best I can do for you. I will put your name on the waiting list. I'll move it as close to the top as I can. You go to the airport tomorrow by 4:00 A.M. That is the last flight to get you out before the deadline. Beyond that, God will have to take over if He wants you to leave."

That night I agonized in prayer. Well before the first rays of morning light began to seep through the window, God had assured me everything was going to work out. "If God wants me to leave Egypt," I told my family, "He will get me on that plane. If not, then surely God is able to open a different door for me."

At the airport I watched the vast number of people milling around. As the plane began to load, I tried to count the travelers; it seemed to me there were more people than could possibly fit into one plane.

When the last ticketed passenger had checked in, the real wait began. A crowd still hovered around the airline counter. The hopeful were clutching their luggage, each one listening for the agent to start calling the standby names. A flight attendant came out, said something to the gate agent, shook her head, and went back to the plane. I continued to pray silently.

Finally a voice called out the name of the first standby passenger who would make the flight: "Michael Amerhome Youssef." I was so overjoyed at hearing my name, I don't remember what, if anything, I said to my family members who had accompanied me to the airport. I do remember running to the gate before the airline personnel could change their minds.

As I thanked the gate agent, he said, "You are one very lucky person, you know that?"

"Lucky?"

"You see those people?" He pointed to at least twenty others waiting for permission to board the flight. "We have only one seat available because of a cancellation. You are so lucky to be at the top of the waiting list."

I took my seat on the plane, knowing I was not lucky at all. I was on that flight to Beirut because God was in control of the circumstances. Not Nasser. Not the Ministry of War Department. Not Egypt Airlines. God was—and is—in control.

"A Man Just Like Us"

From Lebanon I was able to immigrate to Australia, and I eventually came to the United States. This book, however, is not about my life. It is a biblical study of the sovereignty of God, primarily as it is demonstrated in the lives of the prophet Elijah and Queen Esther. But I wanted you to understand from the beginning that the principles from Scripture I will discuss in this book are not just abstractions: They are very concrete, very real, and I have proved them in my life. You can too.

When most people think about Elijah, they consider him to be one of the supersaints of Scripture. It is true that Elijah worked many miracles and had momentous encounters with God. But the Bible clearly states that

> Elijah was a man just like us. He prayed earnestly that it would not rain, and it did not rain on the land for three and a half years. Again he prayed, and the heavens gave rain, and the earth produced its crops. (James 5:17–18)

Most people focus on the last part of these verses in James, the results of Elijah's prayer. They may say, "God does not answer prayer like this anymore," or "I am not one of God's superspiritual servants like Elijah, and that is why God does not answer my prayers."

Both conclusions are wrong. The problem is that most people have never taken the time or the effort to understand how, why, and when God answered Elijah's prayer. I will explore that topic in more depth later.

For now let's focus on the first part of that verse: "Elijah was a man just like us." As we will see throughout this study, Elijah was far from being superspiritual. We will see that he became depressed and discouraged. We will see that he felt scared and frightened. We will see that he doubted and was defeated. In other words, when James said that Elijah was like us, it means he was in every way like us—very human and very vulnerable.

As we go through the biblical account, we will actually discover more about God and how He works than we will about Elijah. We will see evidence of the way God works everything out "in conformity with the purpose of His will." By studying His Word we learn how God deals with His people, how He deals with individuals, and how He deals with nations.

If you want to be effective for God, if you want God to use you in a mighty way, then you must discover how God works. I want to tell you at the outset, though, God is not impressed with what impresses people. God is not moved by what moves people. God does not judge people the way we judge them. God has a different set of criteria by which He works with each of us; each of us is different, and He uses each of us in a different way.

What is common to each of those whom God uses, however, is a willingness to be melted down in service of the kingdom. A wonderful illustration of this principle comes from the life of Oliver Cromwell, who was Lord Protector of the Commonwealth of England, Scotland, and Ireland during the dark days of civil war in the mid-seventeenth century.

During Cromwell's administration, the treasury ran out of silver to mint coinage for the realm. Cromwell sent some of his men to travel throughout the kingdom and find silver for the treasury to use.

The delegation reported back to Cromwell that the only silver they could find was in the statues of the saints in the cathedrals. "What should we do?" they asked their leader.

Cromwell replied, "We will melt the saints and put them into circulation."

In much the same manner, before God can use His man or His woman, before He can put His servants into circulation, He has to put them through a melt-down. I can tell you truthfully that many of God's saints have been sitting in the pews far too long. God cannot make you effective for His kingdom if you are satisfied to be a statue in a cathedral instead of a silver coin in circulation.

God was able to use men like Elijah and women like Esther because they were willing to step forward. They were willing to get out of their comfort zones, willing to be melted down for the Savior's sake.

Let's turn now to Scripture to see how God's sovereign plan for the life of Elijah unfolded. We'll see that when he obeyed God's call to confront a wicked king and queen, Elijah's personal life turned into quite a mess. But part of God's plan included a providential hiding place for His servant. God has such a hiding place for you too.

two

Hidden for God's Purposes

A popular feature in many newspapers is a weekly summary of the plotlines of television soap operas. If they were not such a sad commentary on America's moral decline, these little tidbits would be humorous.

Here is a recent sample of a plotline summary from *All My Children,* a top offering from ABC, the network that declared 1998 "The Year of the Soap":

Brooke was skeptical of Jim's story that a loan shark, whom he paid off with the reward money he got from Dimitri, planted a bomb in Jim's luggage . . . Edmund learned Jim has been telling lies about his past. Allie realized David is out to get Jake after David told Adam that Jake nearly killed him by giving him the wrong medication. Jake told Allie, who had a breakdown, that he loves her . . . Tad came face-to-face with the mystery woman, who broke into his house looking for her necklace. Gillian fumed when she realized Ryan was toying with her. Scott nixed helping Adam get to Liza. Marion threatened Adam in an attempt to get him to divorce Liza.[1]

People have always loved following the twists and turns of a well-plotted tale. The Bible is full of attention-grabbing stories with heroes and villains, intrigue and murder, scandal as well as self-sacrifice. And Scripture does not whitewash the character flaws of some of the main actors of history. Moses, for example, was a hot-tempered murderer. King David was embarrassed by a sexual peccadillo involving another man's wife. Unlike modern soap operas, however, the Bible always keeps these failures in perspective, clearly showing the consequences of immorality and offering redemption from sin.

But let's imagine for a moment that we have uncovered an ancient tabloid with a summary of a drama that occurred around the year 860 B.C. Stripped to its essence, the story might read something like this:

King Ahab continued to claim he is in control of the nation, while conventional wisdom says

Queen Jezebel is the real contender for political power. Jezebel and the government-financed priests of Baal and Asherah have lured many Israelites into the sexual depravity of their fertility cult. But in a dramatic showdown at Mount Carmel, the prophet Elijah called down fire from heaven, then led the people in the mass murder of 850 of Jezebel's priests.

Meanwhile, Ahab sulked over his inability to wrest control of the vineyard next to his Jezreel palace from its owner, Naboth. After the vineyard owner was murdered by a local mob, the sovereign Lord appointed a special prosecutor to investigate whether the king and queen had conspired to obstruct justice by killing Naboth and misappropriating his property . . .

Abuse of power. Sex. Greed. Murder. Conspiracy. Ancient history or today's headlines?

The Prophet from Nowhere

The "special prosecutor" in this imaginary tabloid report was Elijah. God revealed Ahab and Jezebel's sin to His prophet, who then pronounced God's judgment on the wicked king and queen. We will delve into that particular incident in more detail later. Let's begin, however, by looking at the Bible's introduction to Elijah, whose name means "Jehovah is my God."

When we first encounter Elijah, he simply pops up out of nowhere. The Bible does not give his background or his qualifications or his family tree. All we learn is that he was from Gilead. Without further explanation Elijah simply appears on the scene, proclaiming God's word to the king in the royal court.

---

1 Kings 17:1–9

Now Elijah the Tishbite, from Tishbe in Gilead, said to Ahab, "As the LORD, the God of Israel, lives, whom I serve, there will be neither dew nor rain in the next few years except at my word."

Then the word of the LORD came to Elijah: "Leave here, turn eastward and hide in the Kerith Ravine, east of the Jordan. You will drink from the brook, and I have ordered the ravens to feed you there."

So he did what the LORD had told him. He went to the Kerith Ravine, east of the Jordan, and stayed there. The ravens brought him bread and meat in the morning and bread and meat in the evening, and he drank from the brook.

Some time later the brook dried up because there had been no rain in the land. Then the word of the LORD came to him: "Go at once to Zarephath of Sidon and stay there. I have commanded a widow in that place to supply you with food."

King Ahab was probably the most wicked king to rule Israel. (When I talk about Israel here, I am referring to the northern kingdom. After Solomon's reign, the kingdom was divided. The southern kingdom, with its capital at Jerusalem, was called Judah, after the leading tribe of the region. Ten other tribes comprised the northern kingdom, called Israel; its capital was in Samaria.)

Ahab's wickedness was compounded by the fact that he had married a woman who was even more ruthless than he was. The popular image of Jezebel is that of a "painted woman," a seductive and immoral temptress. But Scripture is much more concerned with her role in political affairs and the religious life of the nation than her private conduct.

Another problem plagued Ahab: He was a first-class wimp. Absolutely spineless. Jezebel, who had the superior intellect and greater ambition, did not hesitate to fill the power vacuum in the kingdom. She was a shrewd and calculating manipulator, the power behind the throne.

But of even more importance than all these considerations is the fact that Ahab had married outside the faith. Jezebel was the daughter of Ethbaal, the king of Sidon, a Phoenician city-state. (On today's map, Phoenicia would cover roughly the same territory as Lebanon.) Jezebel's father was not only king of the Sidonians, he was a priest of Asherah, the chief fertility goddess of his people. And Ethbaal had come to the throne by killing his predecessor.

What was Ahab thinking when he married into such an immoral family? Evidently he thought he knew more than his forefathers. Instead of marrying a godly Jewish woman, he entered into a politically motivated union with an idol-worshiping pagan. He probably rationalized his choice of a marriage partner by thinking, *This marriage is a good alliance for the nation. Besides, I can convert Jezebel once she's a part of Israel. I'm the king, so she will have to worship the God of my fathers. I'm sure she will fit right in.*

As a pastor I encounter that kind of muddled thinking all the time. "I'll witness to her. I know I can lead her to the Lord." "He promised to come to church with me, and I'm sure he'll get saved."

That seldom, if ever, happens; it is almost always the other way around. The nonbeliever usually alienates the believer from his faith.

Scripture could not be clearer on this issue. God's

Word says, "Do not be yoked together with unbelievers. For what do righteousness and wickedness have in common? Or what fellowship can light have with darkness?" (2 Cor. 6:14).

This New Testament admonition against a union with nonbelievers was not just intended as a good suggestion; it is a commandment of God. In this verse Paul was confirming what the whole Bible teaches.

Jezebel and Ahab were unequally yoked. She was an intense worshiper of Baal, the supreme god of the Phoenicians. Instead of Ahab converting her, she converted him—along with a significant number of people in Israel. Shrines to Baal started popping up across the kingdom.

Ever since God had brought His people out of Egypt and into the promised land, He had told them to destroy all idols and idol worshipers. But what did the people of God do? They danced with idols. They built shrines to Baal. They disobeyed God—and they suffered dire consequences.

What does the subject of Baal worship have to do with us today? Isn't this just ancient history? Although Scripture, especially the Old Testament, does contain a lot of historical material, it is not just a history book. The stories recounted in the Bible are always told for a particular purpose; there is a lesson—a present-day application—inherent in the text.

Here is the present application, and it is unpleasant, but I say it with some urgency: There is a little Baal in each of our hearts.

A Little Baal in Our Hearts

More than likely you have built a little shrine in some part of your heart. It is a place you have walled off from God, a private place you want to keep strictly to yourself. God wants you to deal with that place. No, God does not want you to pray and fast about it. He does not want you to read books about it. He does not want you to understand how you came to be what you are.

God wants you to exterminate it, whatever it is.

Maybe the Baal in your heart is lust that has not been conquered. Maybe it is a lying spirit that is forever shading the truth. Maybe it is a habit you need to overcome. Maybe it is a relationship that has no place in your life.

Has God been trying to get your attention? Is He saying, "Deal with that little Baal; destroy that private shrine"? If you do what Israel did—keep on tolerating it, keep on feeding it, keep on flirting with it—it could be your undoing.

These little Baals in our lives are like having a gas leak in the house. The pipe leaks just a little bit every day, and you don't realize it. Then one day the leak is ignited and a spark sends the entire house up in flames.

This is what happened in Israel. For years Israel flirted with Baal and the worshipers of Baal. And when Jezebel came from Phoenicia, bringing her fertility cult with her, the whole nation of Israel ignited into immorality.

Elijah was given the awesome task of confronting Jezebel and the rampant immorality and idolatry in Israel. I don't know that I would have easily accepted this responsibility. Elijah had to know that he would pay a price for bringing God's message.

Confronting the Leadership

How did God direct His prophet to confront immorality? Elijah confronted the evil in his society by confronting the nation's leadership. This is an effective strategy, for societies are like fish: They rot from the head down. No home, no business, no organization, no church, no nation will ever rise above its leadership.

Suddenly one day, seemingly out of nowhere, Elijah showed up in the royal palace. He looked King Ahab in the eye and pronounced divine judgment on not only the royal couple but the entire nation: "As the LORD, the God of Israel, lives, whom I serve, there will be neither dew nor rain in the next few years except at my word" (1 Kings 17:1).

The reference to dew may puzzle those who have never lived in an arid climate. Everyone understands the association of the absence of rain with drought, but the effect of no dew is not as obvious. Let me explain.

In the land of Israel, the ground received about one-fiftieth of one inch of dew every morning. This minute amount of dew coated the grass and the plants; it is what gave the foliage life. Without dew there would be no vegetation, and without vegetation, the people and animals would die. So when the man of God said there would be no dew or rain for several years, he was predicting a catastrophic drought.

Why would God choose drought as a method of confronting the nation's leadership? It was a devastating punishment with an unmistakable spiritual significance. God sent this message through Elijah to prove that Jehovah, not Baal, is the living God. The Phoenicians believed that Baal was the source of fertility, that Baal was in control of the forces of nature, and that sacrifices and offerings to Baal would guarantee an abundance of crops and livestock. Elijah's prophecy indicated that God, not Baal, is sovereign over all of creation.

Can you picture Elijah taking this message to the leadership? King Ahab, Queen Jezebel, the members of the court, and the priests of Baal imported from Phoenicia are all gathered in the royal palace. Elijah walks in and makes this startling pronouncement: "There will be no rain or dew in Israel until I say so."

Elijah probably looked and felt completely out of place as he delivered God's message. After he left the others no doubt looked at one another and laughed. "Who is this politically incorrect yahoo?" they hooted.

They were not laughing for long, however. Within a short period of time, they put out an all-points bulletin and launched a nationwide search for the meddlesome prophet, but they could not find him.

Yet notice what the Lord had told Elijah immediately after the prophet delivered His message. God said something very curious. In verse 1 Elijah delivers his message, and in verse 2 God said to him, "Turn eastward and hide in the Kerith Ravine, east of the Jordan."

God had sent Elijah into hiding!

Hidden for God's Purposes

Ahab's network of investigators could not find Elijah because when God hides you, you remain hidden. When God protects you, you are divinely protected. You do not have to be afraid when you are in God's protection program!

Why would God give Elijah a message to preach and then send him into hiding? It does not seem logical. But there is a reason: God's hiding place is always a place of preparation and provision.

It may sound puzzling to us, and Elijah was no doubt confounded with this word from the Lord. Yet as soon as he had delivered God's message, God gave him a new instruction: "Leave this place and hide in the Kerith Ravine."

This new command may have been perplexing, but it was also purposeful. Whenever God is preparing men or women for greater service to come, He invariably sends them to a hiding place.

Let's look at several biblical examples of being hidden for God's purposes.

Joseph had received a vision from God, but he made the mistake of bragging about it to his brothers. Deciding Joseph deserved a comeuppance, they roughed him up and threw him in a pit. Immediately, Joseph went from being the favorite son of his father's house to being hidden in a hole. When a caravan of traders passed by, his brothers sold Joseph into slavery.

Now Joseph was hidden in a foreign country, working as a steward for Potiphar, the captain of Pharaoh's guard. When Potiphar's wife initiated a campaign of seduction, Joseph repeatedly refused her. She took revenge by accusing Joseph of rape, and he landed in prison.

I imagine Joseph was asking the question, "If God is in control, why is my life such a mess?" He had gone from the pit to Potiphar's house to prison. He remained hidden away for *thirteen years.*

Yet God was with Joseph. He kept coming on top. Instead of becoming embittered by slavery, he became Potiphar's most trusted servant and rose to a position of prominence. Even after being thrown in jail, Joseph found favor with God, and prison officials elevated him to an overseer. When he eventually came to Pharaoh's attention, Joseph received the ultimate promotion, becoming the prime minister of Egypt. But God had to hide him—and prepare him—before he was ready for that assignment. In those hiding places God was working out His purpose for Joseph's life.

Joseph and Elijah were not the only two God sent into hiding as part of His sovereign plan. Moses went from the luxury of Pharaoh's palace to a desolate wilderness. God had to hide him before he was ready to lead an entire nation out of slavery and into the promised land.

Esther, a Jewish captive in Persia, was hidden from view in the king's palace. No one knew her true identity until she responded to God's call in a moment of crisis. Why did she remain in hiding for those years? Because God had a plan and a purpose. At the right time He was going to help Esther save her people.

Our Lord Himself was hidden in Nazareth for thirty years until He was fully prepared for His mission. Then the moment finally came when the Father said, "Go now and declare Yourself publicly."

Paul, after his encounter with the risen Christ on the road to Damascus, went to northern Arabia to hide for nearly three years. It was a time of preparation. When Paul was ready, God brought him out of hiding and launched a ministry that quite literally turned the world upside down.

Is there a word for you from the Lord in this? Absolutely!

You may be a mother with young children, and you are feeling hidden from view. Because of your family responsibilities your life seems to consist of one feeding after another, one diaper after another, and you wonder when it is going to end. Providence has hidden you in that place. What is God saying to you? "I am hiding you so I can do something in your life during this time. I am preparing you, and using you to prepare your children, for My purposes."

Perhaps you are a businessman who feels stuck in your job. You long to make a change, but God seems to be hiding you there. Look for His purpose. Discover His plan. Is He preparing you for something? Ask Him to show you.

I do not know what your particular situation may be, but I know this: God will hide you somewhere in the short run until you are ready for what He wants to do in your life. He will let you know when it is time to come out of hiding, and you will be surprised at what God has accomplished in you during this time and what He will accomplish through you in the days ahead.

My Own Hiding Places

I don't want you to think I am just preaching at you, so I will confess that the hiding times in my own life were very frustrating times, and they often seemed to be without merit. But now I look back and see how God was working His purposes out, and I can rejoice.

I'll share one brief example with you. As you know from the previous chapter, I believed at an early age that God had called me to a worldwide ministry based in the United States. But I did not go directly from my native country, Egypt, to the U.S. I first went to Lebanon and then to Australia, where I received my training for the ministry. Australia was my place of preparation, and in many ways it was God's hiding place for me.

Actually, this hiding place turned out to be one of the most wonderful experiences of my life. I received an excellent education, made lifelong friends, obtained valuable ministry experience, and—most important of all—I met and married my precious wife and partner, Elizabeth. I fell in love with this red-haired, green-eyed beauty the first time I saw her. Elizabeth was not only lovely, she was an intelligent, gracious, and godly woman, and I soon learned that God can surprise you with incredible blessings while you are hidden away for His purposes.

Yet Australia was a frustrating place for me as far as my ministry was concerned. No matter how much I enjoyed my work there, I had a gnawing sense— almost a compulsion—that God had something special for me to do, and that I would enter into that special work only after I went to America. So the years I spent in Australia were both delightful and difficult.

If you have not been in a providential hiding place, God wants to send you there. If He would ever use you, He *must* send you there. God wants every one of us, like Elijah, to have a personal Kerith in our lives, because only there will He work out His purpose in us.

At Kerith, God works both inwardly and outwardly. He works outwardly because He has us isolated, with no one else to understand the puzzling frustration of being hidden. Picture Elijah at the bottom of the Kerith Ravine, east of the Jordan. It is a lonely place. The region is quite desolate—nothing but rocks, a few trees, and the bubbling water of a small brook.

Do not underestimate the importance of these surroundings, however. God was working outwardly through them. As Elijah looked at the rocks, he learned about the Rock of his salvation. When he saw the trees, he remembered the words of the psalmist that the tree planted by the water will always flourish. As he studied the bubbling brook, he discovered that out of his innermost being could flow rivers of living water.

Something also happened inwardly while God was hiding Elijah. In verse 1, he is introduced simply as Elijah the Tishbite; but when God brings him out of Kerith and into Zarephath to minister to a Baal-worshiping, Gentile widow, she calls him a "man of God" (1 Kings 17:24).

The process of God's inward working is like peeling an onion. You peel off one layer and the tears flow. Peel off another layer and more tears fall. God will keep peeling off one layer after another because He wants to get down to the real you.

Are you crying and trying to hold on to these layers? Don't! Yes, it can be very painful, but God is removing the outward to reveal the inward. He is not interested in your perception of who you are. He does not care about the public you. God wants to reveal the real you.

As He strips away the layers, God is working out His purposes for your life. He is putting you through a meltdown, so He can put you into circulation. That's what God was doing with Elijah at Kerith. It was only after Kerith that he could move from being Elijah the Tishbite to being Elijah the man of God.

God's Witness Protection Program

God's hiding places are not only places of preparation for service, they are places of provision.

When God sent Elijah into hiding, He had the most unusual resources standing by to meet Elijah's needs. From Scripture, we see that part of this provision was natural and part was supernatural.

At Kerith, God said to Elijah, "Drink from the brook." God had sent him to a place that would (by its nature) protect him from the drought. The brook was God's natural provision for Elijah.

But there was also supernatural provision in store for Elijah. God told him, "I have ordered the ravens to feed you" (1 Kings 17:4). A particular characteristic of ravens makes their appearance here so unusual. Ravens have an enormous appetite—that's where we get the word *ravenous*. These birds eat everything in sight and then some. They are known to starve their young to feed themselves. Yet God used these vultures to bring Elijah bread and meat in the mornings and bread and meat at night. Talk about supernatural!

When you are in God's witness protection program, God can make even the "vultures" in your life—the most mean and godless people—be kind to you and minister to your needs. When you are in God's hiding place, He will hire a supernatural catering service to take care of you.

"I was young and now I am old," the psalmist wrote, "yet I have never seen the righteous forsaken / or their children begging bread" (Ps. 37:25). Are you hidden away for God's purposes? Trust Him to meet your needs. Jehovah-Jireh will provide.

And He will provide an exit from your hiding place, at His appointed time.

When the Brook Dries Up

When it is time, when you are ready, God will bring you out of hiding. And the circumstances may seem as perplexing as those that sent you there.

In Elijah's case, he eventually became a victim of his own success. Scripture says, "Some time later the brook dried up because there had been no rain in the land" (1 Kings 17:7). The drought Elijah prophesied had come to pass, and the brook dried up. Now Elijah was suffering with the rest of the nation.

Have you ever suffered because of your faithfulness to God? Have you ever taken a stand on a difficult issue and had everyone get angry at you? I sure have.

In fact, our church has had an entire denomination become angry at us, because of our opposition to their departure from biblical truth. Eventually, it became obvious that we could not remain affiliated with the denomination because we believed the denominational leadership had denied the authority of the Word of God. Leaving the denomination in which I had been ordained and had served for so many years was a very painful decision. It was painful for our church members, many of whom had spent their entire lives in that organization.

But something I have learned is that most brooks dry up at some point. Business brooks dry up. Relationship brooks dry up. Academic brooks dry up. Denominational brooks dry up. And when that happens, God says, "Don't worry, because I am planning to do greater and better things." Dry brooks do not faze God. He always has a plan!

I challenge you to be willing to go to Kerith and let God work out His purposes for your life. And when your brook dries up, don't panic. He will send you to another place of provision. At the time it may seem as if your life is really a mess, but be assured that God is working behind the scenes, according to His plan and His timetable.

As we will see in the next chapter, God sent Elijah from a dry brook to a Baal-worshiping widow in Zarephath—an unlikely place, but one that turned out to be another place of supernatural provision, a place where God performed the greatest miracle ever through His servant.

three

Faith That Risks Everything

L et's cut through all the talk and get down to the basics." The speaker, Don Taylor, and the other committee members of the Department of Congregations and Development had been listening to me explain my vision for starting a new church in a northwest suburb of Atlanta. "How much is this going to cost the diocese?"

"Nothing," I said, taking a giant step of faith.

Nobody breathed. They just kept staring at me. This was not the way our denomination built churches. The diocese always had to make a heavy financial commitment to support a new work. But in praying and agonizing over starting a church, God had spoken to me that we would not need to ask the diocese for money. I had never started a church before, and I had no idea where the funds would come from, but I knew that God had clearly spoken to me.

"If you approve of my starting a new church," I said, as I let my gaze shift from member to member of the committee, "it will cost you nothing. We only want you to grant us permission."

"We're wasting our time then," Don said. "We have the opportunity to start a new church in an area that needs one, and it won't cost us anything. I'm ready to vote."

The committee gave their unanimous approval.

At that moment I had nothing to offer the Lord except obedience. I trusted that He was in control. He had led me to this point, and He would have to provide.

Our family moved into a house in the area where we wanted to start a church. That necessitated putting our children in private school, which was like striking a match to our entire life savings. But we moved ahead in faith.

As we prayed about facilities to rent for the church—we knew it would be impossible to buy land and build on it for a while—Elizabeth suggested we rent the chapel at this particular private school. Lovett School's chapel seated six hundred people. It seemed like an ideal place.

When I approached the headmaster, Al Cash, about using the chapel on Sundays, he began to question me. "Who are your members? How many do you have?"

"Six," I said, "and they all have the same last name: Youssef."

"You don't have any members other than your family, and you want to rent a chapel that seats six hundred people?"

"That will be all right to begin with." I smiled, realizing my statement would probably blow his mind.

Al shook his head. "That doesn't make a lot of sense—"

"People will come if we have a place to worship. That much I know. And why should you worry about how many people we have as long as we pay the rent?"

Of course, I did not know where the $1,500 per month would come from. But I knew God was calling us to start The Church of The Apostles. And I had a definite assurance that God was going to do something far greater than we expected, in spite of the obstacles we had already encountered and those I knew would lie ahead of us.

"God will provide," I told Al, and I began sharing my vision with him. He became an enthusiastic supporter and helped us negotiate the lease with the school's board.

We did meet many obstacles. We faced financial hurdles, but God took us over them one at a time. We faced relationship hurdles. Some of the friends who had initially said they would help us establish a church later said we couldn't count on them. Many people were skeptical about supporting a preacher with no track record of church building—a preacher who was a foreigner, to boot. But God sent others, some of them not even from our denomination, to replace those who dropped out.

We also faced denominational hurdles. Although we had official approval to start the church, the support was qualified in some quarters; many in leadership were embarrassed by my evangelical convictions. Yet fidelity to the gospel of Christ had been one of the primary motivations for starting a church. And I was not interested in taking any other church's members away. I firmly believed God had called us to evangelize our community, and new converts would be the groundswell for our church.

During those uncertain times, we simply trusted God. On the days when I was tempted to doubt God's calling to build a church, I trusted God. On the days when I did not know whether we could pay our bills or not, I trusted God. On the days when I did not know whether we would have any members or not, I trusted God.

Something my mother had taught me years earlier came to my mind frequently: Do not despise "the day of small things" (Zech. 4:10). Noza Youssef believed that God could take whatever little things we had and multiply them into big things. She imparted that belief to me, and as a result, I risked everything in faith when I heard God's voice.

I believe that any man or woman with Elijah's faith—the kind of faith that is willing to put everything on the line for what God wants to see happen among His people—can make a difference today.

Meeting a Crisis with Faith

Elijah was one solitary man who obeyed God and confronted Israel's immoral and corrupt king. After this experience of prophetic ministry, of declaring God's judgment to the royal palace, Elijah went into hiding at God's command. As we pick up Elijah's story, we now see him confronted by a new crisis: The brook that had sustained him in God's hiding place had dried up. So God directed him to leave at once and go to Zarephath of Sidon. "I have commanded a widow in that place to supply you with food" (1 Kings 17:9).

1 Kings 17:7–16
Some time later the brook dried up because there had been no rain in the land. Then the word of the LORD came to him: "Go at once to Zarephath of

Sidon and stay there. I have commanded a widow in that place to supply you with food." So he went to Zarephath. When he came to the town gate, a widow was there gathering sticks. He called to her and asked, "Would you bring me a little water in a jar so I may have a drink?" As she was going to get it, he called, "And bring me, please, a piece of bread."

"As surely as the LORD your God lives," she replied, "I don't have any bread—only a handful of flour in a jar and a little oil in a jug. I am gathering a few sticks to take home and make a meal for myself and my son, that we may eat it—and die."

Elijah said to her, "Don't be afraid. Go home and do as you have said. But first make a small cake of bread for me from what you have and bring it to me, and then make something for yourself and your son. For this is what the LORD, the God of Israel, says: 'The jar of flour will not be used up and the jug of oil will not run dry until the day the LORD gives rain on the land.'"

She went away and did as Elijah had told her. So there was food every day for Elijah and for the woman and her family. For the jar of flour was not used up and the jug of oil did not run dry, in keeping with the word of the LORD spoken by Elijah.

I often wonder how Elijah reacted to this strange word from the Lord. I probably would have said, "Are You sure, Lord? Did I really hear You right?" I would want to give God a geography lesson. "Zarephath is over seventy miles across the desert, Lord. It's in Sidon, the land of the Phoenicians. It's where the worship of Baal is at its worst!"

God had a purpose, of course, for sending His prophet to Zarephath. He was positioning Elijah for the greatest moment of his life—in fact, one of the greatest moments in biblical history. Elijah did not know that at the time, of course. He simply trusted God to direct him, even if he did not fully understand God's leading.

I have come to realize that when you are in a crisis situation, God's word to you may not seem rational or logical at first. It did not seem logical that God would lead me to build a church with absolutely nothing. Our denomination had never built a church that way, and I had never built a church, period. But that was exactly what God asked me to do. Now I look at our church building, which is probably one of the most visible churches in the southeastern United States, and I am amazed at what God built from that "day of small things."

God does not always ask you to go to places or do things that seem obvious. Elijah must have thought that a seventy-mile hike across the desert was illogical and irrational, but Zarephath was both logical and rational from God's perspective.

Elijah was on King Ahab's most-wanted list. The king was furious with Elijah because Elijah came to the court, announced a drought, and then left. When the drought happened exactly as Elijah had predicted, Ahab wanted to seize God's prophet and kill him.

Where would Ahab's men have looked for Elijah? In all the logical places. They would never have thought to look in Zarephath, a Phoenician city—a city only seven miles away from Sidon, where Jezebel's father was king.

So Zarephath was another hiding place for God's prophet. It was also another place of preparation. The man who would later confront a multitude of Baal's prophets on Mount Carmel was first sent to Jezebel's hometown. God sent him to the very heart of paganism to confront Baal worshipers one-on-one.

There is something else I want you to see about God's choice of Zarephath as the destination for His prophet. Not only does God take you to what seem to be irrational and illogical places, but He often works on more than one front at the same time.

God Works on Many Levels

Some people are brighter than others and have the capacity to do more. They may be able to work on one or two fronts, maybe three, at a given moment. But

God works out His purposes on so many levels at the same time that we cannot begin to fathom it.

Take Elijah's journey to Zarephath. First, there was the obvious purpose of moving Elijah from Kerith to Zarephath simply because the brook had dried up and God wanted to save His servant from starvation. And, as I've mentioned, God was also hiding Elijah from his enemies. But God was working in Elijah's life in other ways that Elijah could never have expected.

On one level, God was showing Elijah that He had a larger purpose for the world than Elijah imagined.

He was giving His prophet a glimpse of the big picture, showing that He is the sovereign God of the universe. God is always working on a larger purpose than we initially realize.

Let me give you another example. Why did God call the Israelites out of Egypt? The obvious reason was to alleviate their suffering as slaves. But He also called them out of Egypt in order to be His ambassadors. We like to think that the Great Commission is found only in Matthew's gospel. But it was first given in Genesis 12:3 when God said to Abraham, "All peoples on earth / will be blessed through you." The reason God called Israel—and the reason He calls you—is to make Himself known in the world.

So when God told Elijah to go seventy miles across the desert to a pagan city, He was working everything out "in conformity with the purpose of his will" (Eph.

1:11). The New Testament gives proof of God's larger purpose in this event. Elijah's seemingly illogical and irrational trip to Zarephath served as the text for Jesus' first public sermon. Let's look at the gospel of Luke, which recounts the first instance when Jesus began declaring His messiahship.

Luke 4:16–30

He went to Nazareth, where he had been brought up, and on the Sabbath day he went into the synagogue, as was his custom. And he stood up to read. The scroll of the prophet Isaiah was handed to him. Unrolling it, he found the place where it is written:

"The Spirit of the Lord is on me,
   because he has anointed me
   to preach good news to the poor.
He has sent me to proclaim freedom
   for the prisoners
   and recovery of sight for the blind,
to release the oppressed,
   to proclaim the year of the Lord's favor."

Then he rolled up the scroll, gave it back to the attendant and sat down. The eyes of everyone in the synagogue were fastened on him, and he began by saying to them, "Today this scripture is fulfilled in your hearing."

All spoke well of him and were amazed at the gracious words that came from his lips. "Isn't this Joseph's son?" they asked.

Jesus said to them, "Surely you will quote this proverb to me: 'Physician, heal yourself! Do here in your hometown what we have heard that you did in Capernaum.'"

"I tell you the truth," he continued, "no prophet is accepted in his hometown. I assure you that there were many widows in Israel in Elijah's time, when the sky was shut for three and a half years and there was a severe famine throughout the land. Yet Elijah was not sent to any of them, but to a widow in Zarephath in the region of Sidon. And there were many in Israel with leprosy in the time of Elisha the prophet, yet not one of them was cleansed—only Naaman the Syrian."

All the people in the synagogue were furious when they heard this. They got up, drove him out of the town, and took him to the brow of the hill on which the town was built, in order to throw him down the cliff. But he walked right through the crowd and went on his way.

In His hometown of Nazareth, Jesus went to the synagogue one Sabbath. He opened the Scripture to Isaiah and started reading a passage about the coming Messiah. Then Jesus said, "Today this scripture is fulfilled in your hearing" (Luke 4:21). The people understood what Jesus meant: "I am the expected Messiah."

Notice what Jesus told them next. "I assure you that there were many widows in Israel in Elijah's time, when the sky was shut for three and a half years and there was a severe famine throughout the land. Yet Elijah was not sent to any of them, but to a widow in Zarephath in the region of Sidon" (Luke 4:25–26).

The people reacted violently to His words. They picked up stones and wanted to kill Jesus. In their narrow-minded self-sufficiency they failed to realize that God loved the whole world, not just the people of Israel. They did not see that God had a purpose for all of mankind, Jew and Gentile alike.

Today many Christians are comfortable living in the buckle of the Bible Belt. We tend to become navel-gazers, as if God is our God alone and He does not care for anybody else. Do you believe that God loves the Hindu? That God loves the Buddhist? That God loves the Muslim? Of course He does. As you are obeying God and working for His kingdom, remember that God may be working on several fronts at once to further His eternal plan. He may have a larger purpose for your life than you can determine at the moment.

God was working on yet another front in Zarephath. He was showing Elijah that He loves Baal worshipers even though He detests Baal. Two years after this episode, Elijah would have a great show-down with the priests of Baal, and he would extermi-nate nearly one thousand of them. But here God was saying, "Elijah, I love these people, and that is why I am sending you to this widow." God wanted to save the widow from starvation as well as Elijah.

Because God is working on these different levels at once, we see only a partial picture. God does not reveal to us His full purpose all at once. But just as His purpose extended beyond Israel when He sent Elijah to Zarephath, we can be sure His purpose extends beyond us. We must look beyond the obvious and the superficial to determine God's larger purpose, because our first impressions of a situation can be misleading.

First-Impression Blues

When you are fully obeying the will of God in your life, one of the greatest temptations you will face is what I call the first-impression blues. Things are not always what they appear to be, and almost never what we expect them to be, when we first encounter a situation.

Elijah experienced the first-impression blues when he arrived in Zarephath after traveling over seventy miles across the desert. He was cotton-mouthed with thirst and starving to death when he reached this smelly, polluted town known for its metalworks. If there had been any truth-in-advertising laws back then, the sign at the city limits would have read: "Welcome to Zarephath, population two—and because of the recent drought, they'll both be dead tomorrow." Elijah must have thought God was playing a practical joke on him.

He saw a woman collecting sticks and asked her for some water and food. She replied, "You don't understand the situation here. All I have left is a little meal and a little oil. I'm going to mix them together, make a fire with these sticks, and bake a cake. After my son and I eat it, we're both going to die."

What Elijah saw first was not what he expected. There was no banner stretching across the road to greet him. The mayor did not shake his hand and say, "Welcome to Zarephath, Elijah. We're glad the Lord brought you here." There was no welcoming committee, no key to the city. And the very person God had sent him to was not receptive initially.

He was suffering from the first-impression blues. The situation seemed impossible. God had told him there was a widow in Zarephath who would feed him. But when he found the woman, her cupboard was bare. She had exhausted her resources; how could she provide for him?

I have to confess that every time I have obeyed God

and stepped out in faith at His direction, I have been through the same process. Fulfilling God's plan for my life, I have moved from nation to nation—first escaping from my home country alone, like Jacob, and later with an ever-increasing number in my household. I faced the first-impression blues in every new location.

When I landed in Beirut, Lebanon, knowing I might never return home to Egypt again, the blues hit hard. I knew few people in the city, and none of them very well. God's sovereign plan had been so clear and my departure from Egypt so dramatic—but now what?

I immediately fell in love with the city, in spite of my apprehension. In 1969 Beirut was one of the most beautiful places in the world. Sheltered on the eastern coast of the Mediterranean, in a picturesque setting of hilly terrain framed by snowcapped mountains in the distance, Beirut was absolutely spectacular. I certainly thought so as I viewed it in the early morning sunlight upon my arrival.

After several hours of searching for a place to stay, I found a bed in a youth hostel. I parked my suitcase there while I went looking for work. Jobs were almost impossible to find, especially for a foreigner. I was young, alone for the first time in my life, and scared.

The money I had brought with me ran out the first week, and I panicked. Succumbing to the first-impression blues is often the result of unbelief, a lack of faith. And as I have learned all too well, first impressions can be wrong. That first week in Beirut, I was trying to do everything on my own, not realizing that God had a "widow of Zarephath" ready to provide for me.

I was naturally shy and had been too bashful to contact any of the few people I knew in the city. One of those people was Maurice Girgis, the evangelist who had led me to the Lord. After several days I worked up my courage and went to see him. A generous man, he introduced me to a pastor named Khaliel Ibrahaim, who invited me to stay in his house for a period of time.

A similar thing happened when I immigrated to Australia. As I prepared to leave Beirut, I knew only one individual in Australia by name. He was a friend of my brother Nathan. I had never met the man, but I wrote to him, asking if he would meet me at the airport. There was not enough time for a reply to my letter, so when I landed in Australia, I did not know if he would be there or not.

I began to search for someone with my name written on a sign. For over an hour I wandered the airport, a stranger in a strange country, struggling to understand the language. I had the grand total of a hundred dollars in my pocket and one small suitcase to my name—and a bad case of the first-impression blues. "I'm in Your hands, God," I said as I looked around the terminal yet again.

"Michael?" asked a man in heavily accented English. "Michael Amerhome Youssef?"

Relief washed over me. It was Nathan's friend.

"I am Wagi Solomon," he said. "I have been looking for you."

"Thank you," I said, and embraced him. Tears filled my eyes as I silently thanked God, who had provided another "widow" for me. Wagi and his wife took me to their home and told me I could stay as long as I needed.

In 1977 my wife and I, along with our oldest two children, left Australia for the United States. Here I was, arriving in another strange land—this time with a wife and two small children in tow—wondering if there would be anyone to meet us. But by then I had learned to trust that God would provide another widow in this Zarephath also. And He did.

If you are striving to obey God's will for your life, you will experience the first-impression blues. It may be in a new job, a new school, a new ministry, or a new relationship. Whatever the situation, put your trust in God. He will always provide widows in your Zarephath.

Beyond the Blues

Elijah did not stay in the first-impression blues. He went beyond the blues, beyond what seemed impossible, and he staked his faith on God's word alone.

When the widow of Zarephath informed him that she was about to use the last of her resources and then face death, Elijah recognized the real problem—her lack of faith—and used it as an opportunity to introduce the woman to God.

Perhaps he said, "No, ma'am, *you* don't understand the situation. You've been worshiping Baal for too long. I want to tell you about Jehovah." He challenged her to put her faith in God, and then to put her newfound faith to the test.

Until you are willing to risk everything in trust of God's provision, you have not learned to live by faith. If everything in your life is calculated, comfortable, and safe, you have not learned what it is to live by faith. By prior experience Elijah had learned to trust totally in God's provision.

Listen to what Elijah told this Baal-worshiping widow. "Before you bake that last cake for you and your son, bake one for me." What was Elijah saying? Was he being selfish? No, he was saying, "Bake God a cake first. Risk your all for the God of heaven. Trust in Jehovah God."

This widow had probably trusted Baal, calling upon Baal and seeking him with all of her heart. But Baal had failed her. Because Baal had let her down, she was now ready to believe in the God of Israel.

Often it is not until people have trusted the god of mammon and become disappointed, not until they have trusted in materialism and ended up in misery, that they are willing to trust in the one and only Savior, Jesus Christ. Many people believe the lie that money and prestige and possessions will make them happy; instead, these things eventually make them emotional wrecks. But some people must get to that point before they will listen to the gospel message.

Most likely that was this woman's condition. She was just desperate enough to listen when God's prophet arrived on her doorstep.

Elijah had already experienced God's supernatural provision at Kerith, when the ravens brought him food every day. But now he was asking a woman he didn't even know, a woman who didn't even believe in God, to risk everything in faith.

It is one thing for you to risk everything in faith; it is another thing to challenge someone else to do it. Some people are daredevils. They take physical risks like bungee jumping and parasailing and skydiving. Some people take financial risks. They invest in new and unproved businesses. They pour themselves into new ventures, and we admire them for it.

When it comes to spiritual risks, however, there are very few takers. That is why the example of Elijah is so important. He was "a man just like us," yet when he prayed, God moved in dramatic ways.

Why did God answer his prayers? Elijah was willing to risk everything on God's promises. He was willing to stand on the word of God alone. And he was willing to tell a starving, Baal-worshiping widow to risk everything on his God, fully believing that God would not let him down.

God Works at Both Ends

Do you know why Elijah was able to do that? He trusted that God was already at work on both ends of the situation. He believed that when God told him to leave Kerith and go to Zarephath, God had already begun to work in the heart of this pagan woman who would provide for him.

When God told Jacob to send his family to Egypt, it was because God had already been working with Joseph.[1] When God told Joshua to send spies to Jericho, it was because God had already been working in the heart of the prostitute Rahab.[2] When God told the Ethiopian eunuch to turn to the book of Isaiah, it was because Philip was already prepared to get into the chariot and help him understand it.[3]

The only way you can risk everything in faith is to believe that God has already been working on both ends of your situation.

Unfortunately, few believers ever understand this. Too many think the Christian faith consists of "give me," "feed me," or "entertain me." But faith is not a matter of stuffing the suggestion boxes with ideas we like and pet peeves we don't like. The world desperately wants to see God's people act with absolute faith in the living God.

What kind of faith risks have you taken that the rest of the world is waiting to see? Elijah met a Baal-worshiping widow and challenged her to give God the last of her food, promising her that God would multiply her resources.

The widow met Elijah's challenge. She, too, risked in faith. And the result of her risking everything in faith was that there was food every day for Elijah, the woman, and her family.

Faith That Risks Everything

How did God do it? How did the flour and the oil continue to multiply? I don't know. The Bible does not tell us. But the God who caused light to flood the universe at His command could speak to the cruet of oil and say, "Let there be oil"—and there was oil.

I must admit there was not much variety. Every day Elijah and the woman's family sat down to biscuits with oil and oil with biscuits. It may have been a boring diet, but it kept them alive through a disastrous drought. God had promised to meet their need, not to give them daily delicacies.

God has promised to meet our needs, too, but He has not guaranteed that He will give us everything we desire or want. Paul did not tell the Philippians, "My God will supply everything that you name and claim." No, he said, "My God will meet all your needs according to his glorious riches in Christ Jesus" (4:19).

Many Christians develop faith formulas, believing they can manipulate God into answering their prayers by saying the right words. Most of their efforts are a waste of time. Faith does not consist of saying the right words in the right way, and God does not respond to formulaic prayers. God responds to faith that is willing to be tested.

While our little faith formulas are futile, there is a formula we can learn from Elijah's faith venture in Zarephath. This formula describes a fundamental principle of God's economy. I express it this way:

Little + God = Much

God can take whatever little things you have—your flour and your oil—and multiply them beyond your wildest expectations. For when God is in it, little becomes much.

Einstein gave the scientific world the first law of thermodynamics, the fundamental principle of a complex universe expressed in the simple formula $E=mc^2$. But Elijah demonstrated this divine formula that defies all scientific laws: Little + God = Much.

How do we develop Elijah's kind of faith? The faith that is willing to risk everything comes out of an intimate relationship with God. It comes from knowing God's Word and knowing how He works. It comes from putting our faith into practice at every opportunity.

Developing an intimate relationship with God, therefore, should be our highest priority. When we enjoy this kind of close relationship, we learn to trust God as our Father—and when our Father promises us something, we take Him at His word.

We should be like the little boy who was standing on a busy downtown sidewalk, right in the middle of the block. He was obviously waiting for something or someone. An older man approached him and asked him what he was doing.

"I'm waiting for the bus," the little boy confidently replied.

The man laughed and said, "Son, the bus stop is in the next block."

"I know. But it will stop for me right here."

The older man tried reasoning with the youngster, who politely continued to insist that the bus would pick him up in the middle of the block.

Finally, the man became annoyed at what he thought was insolence. He raised his voice and said, "You had better start walking if you hope to catch that bus."

As the man started walking off, he heard the screeching of brakes. A bus stopped and the door opened. The youngster started to board the bus, then turned toward the man who had tried to point him to the bus stop.

"My dad is the bus driver," he yelled to the astonished man.

Those who have risking faith are those who know that their heavenly Father will come through for them in ways that seem impossible to the rest of the world.

Do you have risking faith? Or are you comfortable with your calculators and your logic, living only in the realm of the possible? Has God been asking you to walk in faith, while you keep digging in your heels? If God is calling you to take risking faith, respond to Him. Let Him teach you that Little + God = Much.

Elijah put his faith in God to the test, with extraordinary results. But the very next episode in the biblical account shows Elijah's faith put to an even greater test, with an even greater miracle waiting.

four

When Triumph and Tragedy Are Partners

_F_rom my earliest childhood I was the rebellious one. My brothers and sisters were unfailingly polite and unquestioningly obedient. Although I followed our family's Christian tradition, I always felt different.

My rebellion—in dozens of little ways—made me much more difficult to deal with than the other seven children. By the time I was fifteen, my mother was so angry and frustrated with me that she hardly knew what to do.

One day she warned me of my waywardness and my hardened heart. As she spoke, she realized her words were falling on deaf ears.

"You don't listen to what I say, Michael."

"I'm listening." I stood quietly waiting for her to finish preaching to me so I could get out of the house and join my fun-loving friends.

"No, Michael. You hear my words, but you don't listen."

I showed no remorse because I felt none.

In desperation Mother laid her hand on my head and began praying. "Lord, if Michael is not going to be the one to serve You as I have believed all these years, then take him now."

I was shocked. My own mother, who had risked her life to give birth to me, was asking God to take my life if I did not straighten up. For the first time I began to grasp how deeply my disobedience had wounded my parents. The incident did not immediately cause me to change my ways, yet I could not forget my mother's words.

By that time I knew the details of my birth. I had often heard from the lips of my parents that I would grow up to serve God. Even my name—Michael, "messenger of God"—pointed to my destiny as a minister. Perhaps part of my rebellion was that I did not like having my future planned for me.

In the months after my mother's desperate prayer, I began to come around slowly. The turning point came when my brother Samir struck a bargain with me. I was a lackluster student and especially had trouble with math. Samir, who eventually rose to a cabinet-level position in finance in Egypt, patiently tutored me whenever I ran to him for help. He often used my request for help as leverage, making me promise to obey my father or to quit lying to my mother. I was willing to promise anything to get his help; then I usually turned around and broke my promise.

On one occasion he said, "Michael, I will make a bargain with you. I will help you with your math. In return, you will go with me to an evangelistic meeting tonight."

"Certainly, Samir," I agreed readily. "Just help me with these problems and then I'll do whatever you want."

Actually, I had no intention of following through with my agreement, but this time I could not renege as I had done before. Samir made it clear that if I did not go, he would never help me again. I decided it was worth sitting through a boring church service in order to have continued access to his help.

Dreading the ordeal, I decided to bring some of my rowdy friends along. I figured we would laugh during the sermon and make the preacher mad—we had pulled similar stunts before.

I never got around to laughing. The evangelist preached from the Old Testament book of Hosea. He spoke about God's patience with wayward children. I could feel his eyes boring into mine when he warned,

"One day God's patience will run out! A day of judgment is coming, and in that day God's door will be shut. You have a door open today; enter through it."

That night was the first time I really listened to a preacher, and I was the first one to respond to the evangelist's invitation at the end of his sermon. My life was changed forever that night. God had called me from my mother's womb, but I was sixteen years old when I finally surrendered my life to Jesus Christ. That was March 4, 1964.

Four months later my mother was dead.

She had suffered from poor health, and had been in and out of hospitals, for several years. In fact, she was hospitalized in Cairo the night of my conversion. I immediately wrote her the good news of my salvation. She kept my letter under her pillow and showed it proudly to everyone who visited. "Now I can die in peace," she told one visitor.

For a long time after her death, I secretly wondered if my rebellion had caused my mother to get worse and die prematurely. It was a terrible burden for a young person to carry. But I came to realize that God had been in control of the timing of her death. He had sovereignly determined the number of her days. She had been ill before I was born. And in her final bout with illness, God's infinite mercy and grace had sustained her, keeping her alive to witness the conversion of the son for whom she had sacrificed so much and prayed so earnestly.

There are two things I want you to understand from this story. First, notice the sovereignty of God at work. His hallmark is imprinted on all these events—from preventing my being aborted to keeping my mother alive to witness my surrender to His call on my life. God was working everything out in conformity with the purpose of His will. And He can use such seemingly insignificant things as math homework to bring about His divine purpose for your life.

Second, notice the timing of the two events: my conversion and my mother's death. An occasion of great rejoicing and blessing for my family segued straight into calamity and sorrow. This quick succession of God's blessing and life's blasting is not unusual. The highs and lows of life are often close companions. Tragedy and triumph frequently work together as partners.

But ultimately, as we patiently trust God, we experience restoration and resurrection. God can restore order to chaos. He can bring a dying dream back to life. He can heal broken bodies and mend shattered lives.

In a beautiful cathedral in Europe, a magnificent stained glass window towered above the altar. One day a violent storm shattered the resplendent window into a thousand pieces. The church's custodian hesitated to discard the multicolored fragments of glass. Instead, he carefully put them in boxes and stored them in the church basement.

A well-known artist petitioned the trustees of the cathedral for the stained glass fragments. They gave the boxes to him, not knowing his purpose. Two years later the artist invited the church trustees to his studio, where he unveiled his work. To their astonishment, he had re-created the stained glass window, and the restored window looked even more beautiful than the original.

Most of us at some point have experienced the blasting of a storm in the midst of a blessing. If you have been there, or if you are there now, and you have not yet experienced God's restoration work, you will. God specializes in restoring fragments of life into something more beautiful and more meaningful. God brings forth beauty from ashes.

As we turn back to the story of Elijah, this is precisely what we find happening.

From Miracle to Calamity

Remember that we first saw God hiding Elijah at Kerith. God hides us to protect us, to prepare us, and to provide for us. We may resent God's hiding places, but those hiding places are where God works out His purposes in us.

Then we saw how God led Elijah to the Phoenician city of Zarephath, into the heart of Baal worship. The name Zarephath comes from a word meaning "to melt"; the city was known for its metalworking arts. In Zarephath God was purifying His servant by melting away all the dross of the flesh, just as gold is heated in order to burn away all the impurities.

Now we find Elijah still in Zarephath, where God is about to move him from the daily miracle of flour and oil to the testing of calamity and death.

---

1 Kings 17:17–24
Some time later the son of the woman who owned the house became ill. He grew worse and worse, and finally stopped breathing. She said to Elijah, "What do you have against me, man of God? Did you come to remind me of my sin and kill my son?"

"Give me your son," Elijah replied. He took him from her arms, carried him to the upper room where he was staying, and laid him on his bed. Then he cried out to the LORD, "O LORD my God, have you brought tragedy also upon this widow I am staying with, by causing her son to die?" Then he stretched himself out on the boy three times and cried to the LORD, "O LORD my God, let this boy's life return to him!"

The LORD heard Elijah's cry, and the boy's life

returned to him, and he lived. Elijah picked up the child and carried him down from the room into the house. He gave him to his mother and said, "Look, your son is alive!"

Then the woman said to Elijah, "Now I know that you are a man of God and that the word of the LORD from your mouth is the truth."

Elijah, the widow, and her son were all experiencing this daily miracle, a blessing of supernatural provision. No matter how much flour and oil they used, their supply of flour and oil remained constant. The Phoenician woman had risked everything in faith at the challenge of the man of God, and God had come through for her, just as Elijah had promised.

But during this time of miraculous provision, her son became ill and died. The original Hebrew text says, "his soul left him," which lets us know for certain that the boy had truly died and not just lapsed into a coma.

The woman said to Elijah, "What do you have against me, man of God? Did you come to remind me of my sin and kill my son?" (1 Kings 17:18). Her plaintive cry is understandable. Questioning God is a natural response when your life suddenly moves from a miracle to calamity.

A Natural Question

Don't ever allow anyone to send you on a guilt trip for asking the question, "Why did this happen?"

Why is a natural question. The greatest heroes of the Bible questioned God.

When the Midianites were about to decimate Israel, Gideon asked, "Why has all this happened to us?" (Judg. 6:13). Job lost his family, his fortune, and ended up on a heap of rubble. He asked, "Why did I not perish at birth, / and die as I came from the womb? . . . Or why was I not hidden in the ground like a still-born child, / like an infant who never saw the light of day?" (Job 3:11, 16).

Recall the words of the Lord Jesus on the cross. He cried out, "My God, my God, why have you forsaken me?" (Mark 15:34). God's own Son asked questions. So do not feel guilty when you ask God, "Why did this happen?"

There are times in life when the highest of dreams get crushed and the best of hopes are dashed. Sometimes you feel like you're hanging upside down, and your natural question, like this widow of Zarephath, is *why*.

I am convinced that this question must be pounding the doors of heaven from brokenhearted people everywhere. It rises from hospital wards. It rises from lonely bedrooms. It rises from gravesides. It rises from every personal Gethsemane where a troubled soul pleads in private agony.

Understand that I am not talking about the pain that flows from disobedience. I am not talking about the grief that is the natural consequence of sin and rebellion. I am not talking about the normal results of departing from biblical principles. I am talking about being in the middle of God's will, doing God's work the best you know how, when suddenly life's blasting blows you away.

Many Christians understand the paradox of this Phoenician woman, who was experiencing God's blessings in one area, while knowing life's blasting in another.

I have already shared an example of this companionship of blessing and blasting in my own life, at the time of my conversion and my mother's death. I wish I could tell you that blasting was a one-time experience, that once you go through the cycle of blessing and blasting you will never have to go through it again. But that is simply not true. It can happen at any time, and may happen more frequently the more you are doing for God.

In the last chapter I related how God led me to start The Church of The Apostles in the late 1980s. We literally began with nothing and saw God provide miraculously as we struggled to get this new work off the ground. Then in 1990, just as we were experiencing

God's blessing and tremendous growth in the church, our family was suddenly blasted by the storms of life. In a two-week period one of my children landed in the intensive care unit of one hospital, and my wife checked into another hospital for major surgery.

I felt as if the enemy had leveled both barrels of a supernatural shotgun directly at me. I won't share with you how I questioned God during this time; it would not edify you. But I can assure you that God will not only put up with your questions, He will walk you through the emotional minefield.

From Resignation to Anger and Guilt

Emotions are like barometric pressure; they are unpredictable. You cannot trust your emotions.

The widow of Zarephath had been prepared to accept death in the middle of the drought and famine. When Elijah initially came on the scene, she informed him she was about to cook their last meal and then they would die. She was calm and resigned to the coming calamity. But when her son became ill and died, she lashed out in anger, accusing Elijah of coming to Zarephath just to kill her son.

Notice that her anger was directed toward God, but the man of God got the brunt of it. Often when people are angry with God, they take it out on the preacher. When family members or friends get mad at God, they may take it out on the godly person who is nearest to them. Why? Because, like this woman, their anger often is accompanied by guilt.

"Did you come to remind me of my sin and kill my son?" the widow asked Elijah.

Death often brings guilt to the surface. At funerals I have seen people grieve not only for their loved ones, but also for their own sense of guilt and failure in the face of death.

This Baal-worshiping woman did not understand Yahweh. She mistakenly equated Yahweh with Baal. Because Baal was a vindictive god, a god of tit for tat, she thought that Elijah's God was vindictive too. So she assumed that God had killed her son because of her sin.

The young man, however, did not die because of her sin. In the New Testament we find that the disciples once made a similar mistake. They saw a blind man and asked Jesus, "Who sinned, this man or his parents, that he was born blind?" (John 9:2). They jumped to the conclusion that his blindness must have been the result of sin. "Neither this man nor his parents sinned," Jesus answered, "but this happened so that the work of God might be displayed in his life" (v. 3).

We often make rash judgments and imagine a connection between sin and calamity. Instead, we should watch and see how God can use all these things for His glory.

God allowed the widow's son to die in order that He might be glorified. He had been preparing Elijah for this very instance. He had been working out everything in conformity with the purpose of His will, and His intention was to use Elijah to perform the first resurrection recorded in Scripture. The actors in this simple domestic drama were unaware of God's larger purpose behind the events in Zarephath. It was here—not in Jerusalem, or Galilee, or Judea, or Samaria, but in smelly, polluted, pagan Zarephath—that God demonstrated His absolute power over life and death by resurrecting a dead boy.

A Righteous Reaction to Calamity

Elijah, of course, did not know God was about to resurrect the boy. He simply knew that he had persuaded this widow to risk everything in faith, that they had witnessed a tremendous miracle, and that suddenly tragedy struck and he was receiving the blame.

How did God's prophet react to this calamity? What did Elijah do to cause God to perform the very first resurrection recorded in Scripture? We can discover several principles from the biblical account.

1. *Do not defend yourself.* Elijah did not try to defend himself when the woman accused him of killing her son. He did not try to give her a theology lesson or

condemn her false view of God. Instead, he said four words, "Give me your son."

He had just been attacked, assaulted, and reviled. Yet he knew that this was her pain and guilt talking. When people are hurting they often lash out at those who are innocent, sometimes those who are nearest and dearest.

If this happens to you, do not respond emotionally. Do not try to defend yourself. Hold your tongue and take the situation to God.

2. *Question God privately.* Elijah saved his questioning of God until he was alone with Him. The Bible says that Elijah carried the boy upstairs to the room where he was staying. Then he cried out, "Oh, Lord God, why?" Here is that question again! But don't miss this point: Elijah did not ask that question downstairs, where the nonbeliever was struggling with the situation.

Actually, Elijah's initial prayer, recorded in 1 Kings 17:20, is not a good prayer. That verse says, "Then he cried out to the LORD, 'O LORD my God, have you brought tragedy also upon this widow I am staying with, by causing her son to die?'" That was a bad prayer, even though it was Elijah, the man of God, who prayed it. Now he was the one accusing God of bringing tragedy by causing the boy to die, and he was just as wrong as the widow. Elijah was perplexed and agitated. He must have had a deep affection for the boy. But his prayer was wrong.

God is an awesomely good God. And because He is so merciful, He allows us to say some sorry prayers, especially when we are confused and perplexed. When you get frustrated and pray the wrong way, God is not going to get dizzy and fall off His throne. He does not look down from heaven and say, "I'm not going to take any more of these bad prayers." No, God is an infinitely merciful and patient God. If He overlooked Elijah's questions and accusations, He will overlook yours.

3. *Persistent prayer makes a difference.* The third principle we discover in this biblical account is that intense and persistent prayer according to the will of God makes a difference. I do not mean to imply that you may be able to pull off a resurrection. God's power has never diminished, and He is just as able to resurrect the dead today as He was in Elijah's day. But we simply do not see Him working in that way now; evidently it is not part of His sovereign plan for this time in history.

What I want you to see is this: When you have nothing left but God, when you have stripped yourself of everything except God, when you have taken hold of the horns of the altar and persisted in prayer, your prayers *will* make a difference.

4. *Set aside a place to meet with God.* When tragedy struck, Elijah went to the place where he had met God on a daily basis. He went upstairs to the prophet's chamber, the place that had already been sanctified by hours spent in prayer. So when calamity came, he took the calamity to that place.

Do you have a place where you meet God on a regular basis? Do you have a place set aside so that when calamity strikes, when life's blasting blows you away, you know where to retreat?

Notice the intensity with which this man of God prayed in the upper chamber. The Bible says he stretched himself out on the boy three times. Why would he do that? I haven't the foggiest idea. This is the first resurrection recorded in the Word of God. Elijah could not consult a ministry manual and turn to page 197, section B, subparagraph (4): Resurrection of Gentile Boys.

I think he simply did the only thing that occurred to him. The old man was weeping and so brokenhearted that he didn't know what else to do, and he was ready to do whatever it took; if he could somehow pass his own vitality into the boy by stretching out on top of him, then that's what he would do.

There in that room where he had prayed so often, he found the faith to believe God for a resurrection. Scripture says Elijah "cried to the LORD, 'O LORD my God, let this boy's life return to him!'" (1 Kings 17:21). And in this humble home of a Phoenician widow, a Baal-worshiping Gentile, God performed the first recorded resurrection.

God's Response

Notice God's response to Elijah's prayer. The Word of God is so restrained in its account of the incident. "The LORD heard Elijah's cry, and the boy's life returned to him, and he lived" (1 Kings 17:22).

If moviemakers were dramatizing this moment on film, they would probably include thousands of extras. A chorus of angels would sing and trumpets would blow. But that is not the way Scripture presents it to us. There is no showmanship. There are no movie cameras. There are no fund-raising gimmicks. The boy did not write a best-seller about what he saw on the other side of death.

All these things represent man's way. God's way is very simple. One of the popular advertising slogans of our day says, "Just do it." That's the way God works. He just does it. Without fanfare or ceremony God comes on the scene and acts. Similarly, the Word of God records it without elaboration or explanation. It simply says, authoritatively, "God did it."

The Widow's Response

When God answered Elijah's prayer, the Bible says, he "picked up the child and carried him down from the room into the house. He gave him to his mother and said, 'Look, your son is alive!'" (1 Kings 17:23).

How did the unbeliever respond when she received back her son? "Then the woman said to Elijah, 'Now I know that you are a man of God and that the word of the LORD from your mouth is the truth'" (1 Kings 17:24).

She recognized that Elijah was a man of God. She understood that God had done this miracle. She testified to the truth of the word of God. Why? She saw the reality, the intensity, and the integrity of faith under fire.

This woman was honored in the New Testament by being listed in the faith hall of fame with such super-saints as Abraham, Isaac, Jacob, and Moses. Hebrews 11:35 says, "Women received back their dead, raised to life again." This widow, whose name we do not even know, made the roll call of faith for all time when she responded in faith to the living God.

Once Elijah had experienced both tragedy and triumph in Zarephath, after he had loved and confronted Baal worshipers one-on-one, he was ready for his next assignment: the showdown on Mount Carmel with Jezebel and her pagan priests.

five

Stop Wobbling and Take a Stand

*T*he first time I stood on Mount Carmel, I literally had goose bumps. From this 1,800-foot-high peak I not only enjoyed the area's natural scenic beauty, I witnessed an awesome panorama of geography and history.

Facing northwest, I saw before me the port city of Haifa cascading down the mountain toward the sparkling, sapphire-blue waters of the Mediterranean. Off to my right was the ancient fortress city of Acre, the Crusader capital where European knights fought Muslim infidels for control of the Holy Land in medieval times. And here the Ottoman armies stopped Napoleon's military sweep from Egypt through Palestine in 1799.

To my left the majestic mountain fell away to the Plain of Sharon, the fertile coastal region that is the agricultural heart of modern Israel. In this direction lay the seaside city of Caesarea, where Peter baptized the first Gentile convert, Cornelius.[1] Here two successive Roman governors, Felix and Festus, held the apostle Paul under house arrest for two years, until he appealed his case to Caesar and was transferred to Rome.[2]

Behind me was the Plain of Jezreel, another fertile region and one of the most important trade routes in antiquity. Megiddo, strategically situated here at the mouth of the Iron Valley, has been a hotly contested battlefield from ancient times until the twentieth century. And it is the place where, according to some segments of Christianity, the armies of the Antichrist will amass for the final battle of history.

As I stood on Mount Carmel and contemplated all the important historic events these hills have witnessed, I could not help thinking that perhaps the greatest event of all transpired the day one solitary man of God faced off against 850 priests and priestesses of Baal and Asherah, the Canaanite fertility gods. I pictured Elijah in this spot, perhaps hiding behind an outcropping of rock as he waited for the masses of people to assemble. *What was running through his mind?* I wondered. He must have been on his knees, praying, pleading with God for assurance. One thing I know for certain: Elijah would not have dared to propose this confrontation without a clear mandate from the Lord.

On that unforgettable day Elijah cried out a challenge to God's confused people. "How long will you waver between two opinions?" he asked. "If the LORD is God, follow him; but if Baal is God, follow him" (1 Kings 18:21). The literal Hebrew reading of this verse is, "How long will you wobble?" Or, "How long will you walk with a limp?" The people of Israel were wobbling between two opinions. They would not take a stand for either Baal or Yahweh, and Elijah's task was to challenge God's people and confront the false prophets.

Before I recount this dramatic biblical event, I want to share with you why it is important and how it relates to us today. As a pastor I encounter many people who avoid studying the Old Testament because they fail to see how it relates to their lives. To them the Bible stories are no more than boring tidbits of ancient history or tiresome narratives about incomprehensible customs. Yet the Bible is no mere history book or cultural commentary. *All* of the stories in Scripture are there for a purpose. Readers in every generation can find a practical application.

The New Testament confirms that the Old Testament authors recorded these stories for our benefit. "These things happened to" our biblical forefathers,

Paul wrote, "as examples and were written down as warnings for us" (1 Cor. 10:11). That statement gets my attention. Evidently God wanted to warn us about evil things we would face in this world, in order to spare us from physical or spiritual destruction. So God inspired certain men to keep a written record of His dealings with mankind, and this written record serves as a Guidebook for us. Don't you want to be warned ahead of time when danger is lying in wait for you? I certainly do.

When we come to Old Testament stories that seem so strange to us—stories about people worshiping fertility gods in "high places" or slashing their bodies to get the attention of their pagan gods—we must look for the warning God intended for His people. At first glance the warning for our generation may be difficult to discern. After all, we don't engage in these pagan practices anymore—or do we?

Pagan America

In many ways America has become a pagan society. Take one of the practices I just mentioned, bloodletting or ritual cutting of the body. Perhaps you can imagine such a barbaric custom still being acted out in some far-off tribal society—the kind of disturbing image you might expect to come across while thumbing through back issues of *National Geographic*. But would it surprise you to learn that bloodletting as a modern sexual practice is being discussed in university classrooms?[3] And did you know that your tax dollars have sponsored "art" that includes bloodletting?[4]

The National Endowment for the Arts funds museums and theaters like the Walker Art Center in Minneapolis and P.S. 122 in New York City. In 1994 both of these venues featured programs by Ron Athey, a performance artist whose work is a bloody spectacle. In the Minneapolis show, Athey—who is HIV-positive— "cut designs in the back of another man, soaked up the blood with three-ply paper towels," then sent them "sailing over the heads of audience members on a revolving clothesline."[5] Some of the audience members fled in fright or disgust. During the budget battle that ensued in Congress, however, the head of the NEA defended the performance and wondered why much of the public found it so controversial.

Only in America could bloodletting be considered art and not a pagan religious rite. Yet Athey's work clearly shows that his obsession with mutilation has a spiritual origin. In his New York performance, Athey began his "4 Scenes in a Harsh Life" dressed as the famous 1930s evangelist Aimee Semple McPherson. A naked woman, pierced with long needles, stood beside Athey as he described being raised in a pentecostal family and how he came to associate religion with pain and suffering. The next two scenes also contain cutting and slashing, but the final scene includes the exact type of ritual cutting that Elijah witnessed on Mount Carmel.

A critic described Athey's final bloodletting in a review for an arts magazine:

"Dagger Wedding" (Scene IV) was exhilarating and exhausting. Athey, as a sort of minister, presided over the far-from-traditional "wedding" of three women. The brides wore bells on numerous fish hooks that pierced their flesh; Athey wore limes on his . . . Athey administered "communion" (an antiseptic) to each woman . . . Then he quickly and easily inserted a long, thin needle into one cheek and out through the other for all three "brides." The wedding party was joined by five men, also wearing the fish-hook-and-lime ensemble. The ensuing feverish dance caused the hooks to pull and tear their skin, bells and limes gradually dropping off from the force. Cathartic shouts and beating drums carried the performers along, their endorphin high vicariously experienced by the audience. Shock value aside, the performers' endurance of pain was oddly inspirational.[6]

What I find much more shocking than a bloodletting ritual performed on the American stage is the fact that serious art patrons found it "oddly inspirational."

Granted, only a small minority of the population would ever engage in such a practice—or pay good money to see someone else do it—but consider the other pagan practice I referred to earlier: worshiping the gods and goddesses of the fertility cult. Although we call it something else, the modern fertility ritual has become just as widespread—and just as dangerous spiritually—as it was in Bible times.

The Gods of Materialism

In the agricultural society of Old Testament times, fertility rituals were associated with the desire for wealth. The Canaanites, and the Israelites who abandoned Yahweh, sacrificed to Baal and Asherah to ensure an abundant harvest, which would mean financial prosperity.

Some of the fertility rituals included gross immorality and sexual perversion. But under Jezebel's leadership, morality was out and prosperity was in. Ahab was so busy worrying about the nation's economy, not to mention his own personal wealth, that he could not be bothered with old-fashioned notions of morality and character. His political advisers had probably made a sign for his palace office that said, "It's the economy, stupid."

Materialism has always beckoned attractively to the people of God. In Baal they thought they had found a shortcut to prosperity. They imagined they could get a financial blessing without having to be obedient to God's commandments.

God's people are no different today, which is why the health-and-wealth teachers have been able to take the entire gospel hostage to the doctrine of prosperity. God *has* promised to bless His people. But, as we will see in the next chapter, these are conditional promises. We cannot command God to prosper us; we can, however, meet His conditions for receiving a blessing.

Jesus taught succinctly against the worship of materialism. He said, "No one can serve two masters. Either he will hate the one and love the other, or he will be devoted to the one and despise the other. You cannot serve both God and Money [or *mammon* in the King James]" (Matt. 6:24).

Mammon is a variant of a common Aramaic word referring to riches or wealth of any kind. Jesus always used it derogatorily, to show that His followers should not put their trust in wealth or riches or anything of temporal value.

I cannot help but note the irony that the quintessential "material girl," Madonna, is named after the mother of Jesus—a woman who was the complete antithesis of everything this poster child for self-indulgent sensuality stands for. Yet rock stars and movie stars and overpaid athletes are adored by millions of fans who care nothing about morality or righteousness. These celebrity superstars are our gods and goddesses of materialism, our very own all-American fertility cult.

Again, the same attitude pervades Christianity. We have our own celebrities, our own superstars, our own television personalities. And most believers long to live the lifestyles of the rich and famous, not the holy lifestyles of the not so rich and much more obscure people such as the ministers and missionaries who give their lives to the gospel of Christ.

I do not mean to imply that holiness is equated with poverty or that wealth is always ungodly. I am simply pointing out that the accumulation of possessions is not to be our goal. Prosperity is not to be our preoccupation. Wealth is not our security.

Yet instead of confronting materialism, much of the church has embraced it.

Conformity Instead of Confrontation

I am convinced that history will attest to the fact that much of the moral and ethical breakdown in our great nation is due to the fact that some time ago we chose conformity instead of confrontation. We chose consensus instead of conviction. We have followed public opinion polls instead of obedience to God and His laws.

Americans seem to be addicted to public opinion polls, and the news media feed us a steady diet from the pollsters. As I write this chapter, President Clinton has been embroiled in a number of scandals. The latest polls show that a majority of people believe the president lied under oath—that he committed perjury—but a majority also approve of the job he is doing as president and want him to stay in office. Morality has been shoved aside in favor of pocketbook politics. "As long as the economy is good, don't bother me with moral issues," the average voter says.

Rather than confronting sin and immorality, the Christian community is conforming more and more to the society at large. Divorce and adultery are becoming as widespread among church members as among nonbelievers. It is no longer unusual to find child abuse or sexual abuse occurring in church families.

The church is becoming a mere reflection of society, with fewer and fewer people loving God, serving Him, or making Him known. The Sunday morning worship service has turned into a spectator sport. People show up to be entertained by the musicians and the pastor. Most of the congregation do not want to participate or to make any kind of commitment. They are content to sit in the pews, much the way they sit in front of the television set.

A prominent coach once described a football game as an event where fifty tired people who are in desperate need of rest are playing on the field while being watched in the stands by fifty thousand resting spectators who are desperately in need of exercise. A football game cannot be won by the spectators, and neither can the race the Christian is called to run.

As we turn now to the centerpiece of the life of Elijah—the confrontation with a multitude of pagan prophets—we find him in hand-to-hand combat, while the masses of the people of Israel, standing there atop Mount Carmel, were indifferent and skeptical spectators. Baal had been winning over Yahweh in the public opinion polls. The people were wobbling and refusing to take a stand for the God of their fathers, the God of Abraham, Isaac, and Jacob.

---

1 Kings 18:1–2, 17–40

After a long time, in the third year, the word of the LORD came to Elijah: "Go and present yourself to Ahab, and I will send rain on the land." So Elijah went to present himself to Ahab . . .

When [Ahab] saw Elijah, he said to him, "Is that you, you troubler of Israel?"

"I have not made trouble for Israel," Elijah replied. "But you and your father's family have. You have abandoned the LORD's commands and have followed the Baals. Now summon the people from all over Israel to meet me on Mount Carmel. And bring the four hundred and fifty prophets of Baal and the four hundred prophets of Asherah, who eat at Jezebel's table."

So Ahab sent word throughout all Israel and assembled the prophets on Mount Carmel. Elijah went before the people and said, "How long will you waver between two opinions? If the LORD is God, follow him; but if Baal is God, follow him."

But the people said nothing.

Then Elijah said to them, "I am the only one of the LORD's prophets left, but Baal has four hundred and fifty prophets. Get two bulls for us. Let them choose one for themselves, and let them cut it into pieces and put it on the wood but not set fire to it. I will prepare the other bull and put it on the wood but not set fire to it. Then you call on the name of your god, and I will call on the name of the LORD. The god who answers by fire—he is God."

Then all the people said, "What you say is good."

Elijah said to the prophets of Baal, "Choose one of the bulls and prepare it first, since there are so many of you. Call on the name of your god, but do not light the fire." So they took the bull given them and prepared it.

Then they called on the name of Baal from morning till noon. "O Baal, answer us!" they shouted. But there was no response; no one answered. And they danced around the altar they had made.

At noon Elijah began to taunt them. "Shout louder!" he said. "Surely he is a god! Perhaps he is deep in thought, or busy, or traveling. Maybe he is sleeping and must be awakened." So they shouted louder and slashed themselves with swords and spears, as was their custom, until their blood flowed. Midday passed, and they continued their frantic prophesying until the time for the evening sacrifice. But there was no response, no one answered, no one paid attention.

Then Elijah said to all the people, "Come here to me." They came to him, and he repaired the altar of the LORD, which was in ruins. Elijah took twelve stones, one for each of the tribes descended from Jacob, to whom the word of the LORD had come, saying, "Your name shall be Israel." With the stones he built an altar in the name of the LORD, and he dug a trench around it large enough to hold two seahs of seed. He arranged the wood, cut the bull into pieces and laid it on the wood. Then he said to them, "Fill four large jars with water and pour it on the offering and on the wood."

"Do it again," he said, and they did it again.

"Do it a third time," he ordered, and they did it the third time. The water ran down around the altar and even filled the trench.

At the time of sacrifice, the prophet Elijah stepped forward and prayed: "O LORD, God of Abraham, Isaac and Israel, let it be known today that you are God in Israel and that I am your servant and have done all these things at your command. Answer me, O LORD, answer me, so these people will know that you, O LORD, are God, and that you are turning their hearts back again."

Then the fire of the LORD fell and burned up the sacrifice, the wood, the stones and the soil, and also licked up the water in the trench.

When all the people saw this, they fell prostrate and cried, "The LORD—he is God! The LORD—he is God!"

Then Elijah commanded them, "Seize the prophets of Baal. Don't let anyone get away!" They seized them, and Elijah had them brought down to the Kishon Valley and slaughtered there.

———

We read at the beginning of 1 Kings 18 that God told Elijah to go and present himself to King Ahab. Remember, there had been a severe drought for three years, as Elijah had prophesied. At the end of that time, God announced to His prophet that He was now ready to end the drought, and once again He sent Elijah to confront the politically correct, weak-willed king.

Ahab was the champion of pluralism. This wimp of a king had compromised his faith and allowed his wicked, godless queen to desecrate the nation by entertaining 850 prophets of Baal and Asherah—at the taxpayers' expense. Yet when trouble came, the king blamed Elijah for the nation's disasters. After a three-year drought, everything had turned to dust. No crops. No vegetation. No food. The country was facing a catastrophe.

Notice the irony here. King Ahab and Queen Jezebel had been worshiping Baal while paying lip service to the one true God, Yahweh. Why were they worshiping Baal? Because Baal was the god of fertility, the god who was supposed to ensure an abundance of crops and a bountiful harvest. Yet when the drought came, Ahab did not count it as a failure of Baal. He blamed the man of God, calling him "the troubler of Israel."

When a nation's leadership leads into compromise, the public becomes confused. That is what was happening at this point in Israel's history, when all these confused people gathered atop Mount Carmel to witness Elijah's confrontation with the prophets of Baal and Asherah. We know they were confused, because the Bible says they were halting between two opinions. They did not worship Baal alone; they did not worship Yahweh alone; they tried to compromise, and the result was utter confusion.

I don't like debating people when it comes to the faith. I don't believe the gospel is to be rammed down people's throats or argued about. Jesus said, "I am the only way to heaven. You can't go to heaven with your good works, or your money, or with anything else except Me."[7] So I tell people, "If you want to go to heaven, accept Jesus Christ. If you don't want to go to heaven, reject Him." It's that simple. I don't have to argue the point.

That's what Elijah said on Mount Carmel that fateful day. He was calling the people to make a decision between two extremes. "If the LORD is God, follow him; but if Baal is God, follow him" (1 Kings 18:21).

Today when someone takes a stand on a moral or spiritual issue, he is called an extremist. I am not talking, of course, about those who justify using violence to make a moral statement. Those who bomb abortion clinics or shoot abortionists are just as guilty of murder as those who abort babies. I am referring to our national abhorrence of anyone who is not afraid of speaking out on moral issues.

Let me return to a previous example. After months of the Monica Lewinsky scandal, opinion polls showed that most Americans believe Bill Clinton lied under oath in his deposition in the Paula Jones case, but they also give him high approval ratings as president. When someone dares to speak out and say that if it's true, if the president really did commit perjury, then perhaps he is not morally fit to hold high office, there is an outcry—not against a politician who may have subverted justice and violated the trust of the electorate, but against the person who dares to point it out. The person who takes a moral stand is considered an extremist.

I pray that God will raise up more extremists! Let me tell you, on the authority of Scripture, that God wants people to be at one extreme or the other. Jesus told the church at Laodicea, "You make me sick. You make me so nauseous, in fact, that I want to vomit."[8]

Why did the Laodicean church make Him sick? Because they were middle-of-the-roaders on every issue. They straddled the fence and sought to please everybody. They wanted to play footsie with sin during the week and go to church on Sunday. They wanted to identify with society's immorality and still call themselves religious.

Jesus told them to quit wobbling and take a stand. "I'd rather you be hot or cold than to stay lukewarm," He said. Being moderate may be admirable to the secular media, but it is not very exciting to God.

You don't need a Ph.D. to know that people pleasers end up pleasing no one. Compromise produces confusion.

Indecision creates turmoil. James wrote that a double-minded person is unstable.[9] Quit wobbling between two positions. Quit worrying about what people think. Be concerned most with what God thinks. Take a stand!

Elijah Took a Stand

Elijah took a stand for God at the very moment when it was most difficult. Elijah remarked to the people on Mount Carmel that he was outnumbered. But he wasn't just outnumbered, he was the only one standing on Yahweh's side.

For most of us, being outnumbered two to one would be terrible. Twenty to one would be a disaster of epic proportion. But to be outnumbered 850 to one seems utterly impossible. To have 850 people telling you that you are wrong is inconceivable. But that is where Elijah was, standing alone in front of the leadership of the country.

What did it mean for Elijah to be outnumbered to that extent? It meant that all the odds favored Baal. But the outcome was not dependent on who had the most people on their side. The central term of the contest was that the god who acts is God.

Can you imagine these confused Israelites coming to the top of the mountain, then standing there and watching the spectacle? I imagine them to be like the religious people of our day—those who go to the apostate churches, who believe that there is a God but that He is a million miles away. They believe that Jesus died on the cross, but His death and resurrection are totally irrelevant and divorced from their daily lives. They go to church once a month to get a fix of religion, but they also read their daily horoscopes, just to be sure. Imagine these religious people standing there, wide-eyed, watching for nine hours while hundreds of false prophets called upon Baal with no response.

I think the prophets of Baal sincerely believed their god would hear them. How disappointed they must have been. There is nothing worse than being sincerely wrong. After several hours they must have begun to realize that they had been deceived and deluded.

When the 850 prophets could not get Baal to hear them, they started dancing around the altar they had made. They were gyrating and gesturing frantically to get Baal's attention, but to no avail. Finally, when they got really desperate, they began to cut themselves with knives, hoping to provoke Baal's response. But that was futile too.

I can't help wondering what King Ahab was thinking while this bloodbath was going on. I imagine he was thinking of some choice words, words he would never dare speak to his wicked wife. "Jezebel, you told me that Baal was the real thing! All your opinion polls said that Baal was powerful, that he was in charge of nature. What have you got to say for your god now?"

Elijah had told the crowds, "You call on the name of your god, and I will call on the name of the LORD. The god who answers by fire—he is God" (1 Kings 18:24). They called on Baal all day long. But Baal could not answer, and Elijah knew it.

Our circumstances are so different today, yet we respond in exactly the same way. We are forever studying public opinion polls and then formulating our position. We look at what others are doing and then decide we will do the same thing. It does not please the Lord when we follow public opinion rather than obeying the Word of God.

Let me ask you something. Do you spend as much time consulting the Word of God as you do reading the newspaper or watching television? Do you follow the crowd, or do you seek to hear from God and follow only Him? Does God honor your trust in Him and answer your prayers when you pray in accordance with His will?

We all put our trust in something or someone. If you put your trust in material things and your children are empty, can your materialism fill them? Absolutely not. Your material possessions will stand in mockery against you, because they cannot answer.

Do you worship a god of rationalism that says "I think, therefore I am"? When you confront a tragedy in life, can your god answer with the peace that passes understanding? No. Your rationalism will only mock you; it cannot answer you.

Is your god sensuality? When you come to the end of your life and feel your own mortality, you can cry out to sensuality. But when passion's flames have become dust and ashes, sensuality will not answer you.

But there is a God who will answer, and you can know Him. Elijah showed us how God answers.

Late in the day, when the Baal worshipers finally grew weary and hoarse, Elijah said, "Come near. Let me show you how my God works." There was no hocus-pocus, no smoke and mirrors, no sleight of hand on Mount Carmel that day. There was simply one man who knew how God works.

As the sun was sinking like a blazing lead ball into the Mediterranean, Elijah took twelve stones, representing each of the twelve tribes of Israel, and he repaired the altar of God. Repairing the altar was necessary because it had crumbled out of neglect and disinterest. The people had been so busy running after other gods, they had not cared that God's altar had been torn down.

How is your family altar? Is it in disrepair out of negligence? How is your prayer life? Have you been too busy with other things? You must repair the altar before God can answer.

Once he had repaired the altar, Elijah did something

very curious to the wood he had placed there. In contrast to the dry wood the prophets of Baal used, Elijah saturated his wood with water. Because of the drought, the water had to come from the Mediterranean. So the people Elijah called on to assist him had to carry all those barrels of water from the sea up to the altar, a place about 1,500 feet up the mountain.

After they poured twelve barrels of water out, saturating the wood, Elijah sent them back for four more barrels. Why did he soak the wood and make a trench of water around the altar? He wanted to give all the odds to Baal and all of the handicap to Yahweh. Therefore, when God answered there would be no mistaking that it was His response.

Some knuckleheaded liberal commentators have said that Elijah must have had a magnifying glass to concentrate the rays of the sun, thus causing a fire. That cracks me up. In the written record of this account, the Holy Spirit emphasized two facts: The wood was thoroughly wet, and it was sundown. There was not enough sunlight left to spark a fire, even if the wood had been dry.

When Elijah was satisfied that the wood was soaked, he offered a short prayer. Immediately fire fell from heaven and consumed the sacrifice. "The god who answers by fire—he is God."

Note the sharp contrast. Elijah did not have to cut himself or shout to God for hours. Everything he did—

repairing the altar, wetting the wood, filling the trench around the altar—had been in perfect obedience to the Lord.

So when he prayed publicly, he only prayed a few words. But consider this: Elijah had been praying privately for three years. All that time, hiding in the Kerith Ravine and in Zarephath, God had been preparing him for this moment.

We often underestimate the importance of God's preparation in our prayer lives. We think that if we can just come up with the right words, God will answer our prayer. But it is not the eloquence of your speech God considers; He is looking at the condition of your heart. And it is not the length of your prayer, but the strength of your prayer that matters. It is not the economy of your words in public prayer, but the intensity of your private prayer that will cause God to answer by fire.

A Moment in Salvation History

By now you may be asking, "Why doesn't God work that way today? Why doesn't He send fire from heaven anymore?" Perhaps you imagine confronting the mayor of your city. "Your Honor, bring your bull to the altar and I'll call down fire from heaven." That would get everyone's attention, all right.

But you have to understand that Mount Carmel

was a moment of time in salvation history, a moment where everything was at stake. Abraham, Moses, Joshua, David, the kingdom—everything hung in the balance.

God does not work so dramatically most of the time, not unless it is an absolutely decisive moment of critical, world-changing significance. Our sovereign God responds in the manner He deems appropriate for the situation, and we cannot command Him to perform as we see fit.

When fire came down from heaven and burned everything in sight, the spectators on Mount Carmel fell on their faces and cried, "The LORD—he is God! The LORD—he is God!" (1 Kings 18:39). No longer could they wobble between two opinions. It was a decisive moment in the history of the nation of Israel, and by extension, in the life of the church.

But as great as this event was in biblical history, we do not look back to Mount Carmel for salvation. Why? Because we have a better example. We look back to Calvary and to the empty tomb. We look to the Upper Room in Jerusalem, where the Holy Spirit descended on the first believers.

When fire fell from heaven on the day of pentecost, men and women were changed forever, filled with the power of the resurrected Christ. We do not look back to the fire that consumed stone and wood and even water, but to the fire that cleanses us and purifies us. We do not look to the fire that consumed the sacrifice, but to the fire that consumes us with zeal to declare to the world that Jesus is Lord.

How does God convince America that He is the Lord of all? He wants to do it by your deeper and purer inner fire, the flame that enters in and burns the dross of compromise in your life, the flame that burns indecision and indifference out of your life, so that you are able to confront the world.

Perhaps you are to confront just one person with the claims of Christ. God wants to do it through a perceptible change in your life. He wants people to look at you and say, "Why are you different? Why do you have hope?"[10] He wants us to display His power in our daily living, so that we do not live by sight like the rest of the world, but we live by faith, seeing the unseen. God confronts the world when His church exhibits such unity of spirit that people are compelled to say, "Behold, how they love one another."[11]

If we know that God confronts the world by our zeal and love for the lost, then how should we respond? That God called Elijah to confront 850 false prophets at once does not mean He necessarily wants you to do the same. God calls some as evangelists to reach the masses. But He calls every believer to confront the enemy, Satan, by confronting one person at a time. Simply ask God what one person He wants to win through your witness. Say to Him, "Lord, lay some person on my heart, so I can pray for that person's salvation."

Then the moment comes that God provides, not by your engineering but by His sovereign grace, for you to confront that one person. And how exciting it is to watch God send the fire of salvation from heaven for that one person!

I hope my words have challenged you to quit wobbling and take a stand for Christ. One of the important lessons you will need to learn in order to take a stand is how to cling to the promises of God. Let's turn to that topic now.

six

Clinging to the Promises of God

*C*hristians who do not know how to appropriate the promises of God remind me of a story about Crowfoot, the great chief of the Blackfoot confederacy in southern Alberta, Canada. When Crowfoot gave the Canadian Pacific Railroad permission to cross tribal land from Medicine Hat to Calgary, the railway commission wanted to do something special for the chief. So in return for his gracious act, Crowfoot received a lifetime railway pass, which he could use anywhere in Canada.

Crowfoot treasured the pass. He put it in a leather case and proudly wore it around his neck for the rest of his life. Yet there is no record that the chief ever once availed himself of the right to travel on the Canadian Pacific Railroad.

Tragically, many Christians treat the promises of God the same way. They may hang them on the walls, they may recite them to their children, they may believe them in their heads—but they do not know how to appropriate God's promises.

Think of it this way. If you give me a check and I never deposit it or cash it, the check is useless to me; I never appropriated your gift. Similarly, the Holy Spirit has given us promises: They are recorded in God's Word. But what you do with these promises, how you apply them in your life, is up to you.

Why do believers fail to understand how to apply God's promises to their lives? To begin with, many people have difficulty believing the scriptural evidence that God is faithful to His promises and will never go back on His word. For example, Psalm 145:13 says, "The LORD is faithful to all his promises." But because the scourge of our generation is the ease with which promises are made and broken, some Christians have trouble taking God at His word.

In days gone by, people thought long and hard before they made a promise because they intended to keep it, even at a personal sacrifice. There was a time when a man's word was his bond. But today we make fleeting promises, then tomorrow we say, "Well, I'm sorry, I just couldn't do it." And because we get away with not keeping our word, we think it's all right to break our promises.

In America, the public arena has become a truth-free zone. All too often the words "campaign promise" indicate something a candidate says simply to get elected, not a pledge he intends to keep. The old adage that politicians spend half of their time making promises and the other half making excuses is no longer humorous; it is too close to reality.

Did you ever think that promise-breaking would become such an epidemic that a national ministry would be raised up just to motivate men to keep the promises they have made to their wives and children? The tremendous response to Promise Keepers indicates just how pervasive the problem has become.

How I thank God that He does not make frivolous promises that He does not intend to keep. God is faithful to *all* His promises, just as Scripture says. In the past thirty-odd years I have experienced His faithfulness over and over. And I have learned firsthand that there is one thing that God cannot do, and that is not keep His promises.

God's promises may not be fulfilled exactly the way I want them to be, or at the time I want them to be, but He always keeps His promises.

Let's look again at the biblical record and see how Elijah clung to the promises of God. There are two principles we need to learn about God's promises first, however. One principle is that some of God's promises are conditional and others are unconditional; the second is that some promises are universal and some are personal.

The Nature of God's Promises

An unconditional promise is not dependent on our actions; its fulfillment is strictly up to God. For example, God promised the land of Israel to the descendants of Abraham, Isaac, and Jacob. It was an unconditional promise. Even after four hundred years of slavery in Egypt, God still kept His promises and led them into the promised land.

A conditional promise, however, has a condition attached to it. In other words, it depends on us to do something in obedience to God before the promise can be fulfilled. "If you will do this," God says, "then I will do this."

An example of a conditional promise is this familiar passage in 2 Chronicles: "If my people, who are called by my name, will humble themselves and pray and seek my face and turn from their wicked ways, then will I hear from heaven and will forgive their sin and will heal their land" (7:14).

"If . . . then." When God's people meet the condition, God fulfills the promise.

The second principle relating to the nature of God's promises is that some are personal and some are universal. A personal promise is limited to one person at one particular time. A universal promise has no limitations and no expiration date; it is for all believers in all time periods.

As we get back to our story of Elijah, we must examine the nature of God's promise to His prophet. God's promise to withhold rain and then send rain at Elijah's word was a personal promise. God never made a universal promise that believers could decide whenever they wanted it to rain and He would be obligated to open the floodgates. I certainly believe in praying for rain when you are suffering from drought conditions, but that is praying for God's gracious provision in a time of crisis; we do not have a general promise that we can call down rain whenever we want it.

We get into trouble when we make personal promises to be universal promises. In Mark 16, for example, Jesus made a personal promise to the disciples for a definite time about picking up snakes and drinking poison (vv. 17–18). The purpose of His promise was for the protection of the disciples as they began the task of evangelizing the world. Yet some uninformed, misguided souls have claimed this promise universally and made snake-handling a regular part of their worship service. They are wrongly putting God to the test, and He is not obligated to protect them from the dangers of handling poisonous snakes.

God's promise to Elijah was not only personal, it was also conditional. When Elijah obeyed God, meeting the condition for the promise, then God fulfilled it.

Here is how it transpired.

Immediately after God's incredible intervention on Mount Carmel, when the fire fell from heaven and supernaturally consumed everything in sight—stones and wood and sacrifice and water—Elijah told King Ahab to get home quickly because rain was in the forecast.

---

1 Kings 18:41–46

And Elijah said to Ahab, "Go, eat and drink, for there is the sound of a heavy rain." So Ahab went off to eat and drink, but Elijah climbed to the top of Carmel, bent down to the ground and put his face between his knees.

"Go and look toward the sea," he told his servant. And he went up and looked.

"There is nothing there," he said.

Seven times Elijah said, "Go back."

The seventh time the servant reported, "A cloud as small as a man's hand is rising from the sea."

So Elijah said, "Go and tell Ahab, 'Hitch up your chariot and go down before the rain stops you.'"

Meanwhile, the sky grew black with clouds, the wind rose, a heavy rain came on and Ahab rode off to Jezreel. The power of the LORD came upon Elijah and, tucking his cloak into his belt, he ran ahead of Ahab all the way to Jezreel.

Scripture paints a magnificent word picture in this passage. Elijah tells Ahab that there is "the sound of a heavy rain" (1 Kings 18:41). The original language literally says, "I hear the feet of rain approaching." Elijah heard the sound of rain running toward them. I don't know if Elijah heard it by faith, or if he heard it literally. It doesn't really matter. The important thing is that he knew that rain—a whole lot of rain—was about to fall.

The Bible says that Ahab descended the mountain to eat and drink. But where did the man of God go? He climbed to the very top of Mount Carmel to kneel on the promises of God. Elijah went up to pray, because when he heard the sound of rain there was not a single cloud in the sky.

Why, then, did Elijah confidently tell the king there was about to be a downpour? Because he had just met God's condition for the fulfillment of the promise. When Elijah was still in Zarephath, at the widow's home, God had said to him, "Go and present yourself to Ahab, and I will send rain" (1 Kings 18:1). That was the condition for rain. God was saying, "Elijah, if you do that, I will send the rain." Remember, it had not rained for three and a half years.

When Elijah confronted Ahab and Jezebel and the 850 prophets of Baal and Asherah, he met God's condition. Elijah's obedience was about to bring the fulfillment of God's promise, and that's why he told Ahab to prepare for a deluge.

Meeting God's Conditions

So many of the promises in Scripture are conditional promises. I get frustrated when I see believers who are confused about this issue. Most Christians today love to claim the promises, and multitudes are following the "name-it-and-claim-it" preachers, who have centered their entire ministries on claiming promises.

But when a person claims a promise—without understanding its conditional or personal nature—and then nothing happens, she feels devastated. Then the brokenhearted Christian asks, "What happened? Why didn't God answer my prayer?" Sadly, some people have had their faith shattered because they have not understood the biblical principles involved. They have tried to appropriate God's promises in error, either claiming a personal promise that was never intended to apply to them, or not realizing that the promise they claimed was contingent on their meeting God's conditions for the fulfillment of that promise.

If God's promise is conditional, you cannot escape the conditions. God must be true to His Word. He set these things in motion, and He is not going to change His mind. So if you want to receive the promise, you must meet God's conditions.

Not only must you meet God's conditions, you must wait for His timing. The Bible says that you will reap what you sow. A farmer who plants corn is going to harvest corn, not wheat or oats or rye. What you sow is what you reap—in due season.

> Do not be deceived; God cannot be mocked. A man reaps what he sows. The one who sows to please his sinful nature, from that nature will reap destruction; the one who sows to please the Spirit, from the Spirit will reap eternal life. Let us not become weary in doing good, for at the proper time we will reap a harvest if we do not give up. (Gal. 6:7–9)

There is a waiting period between the time you sow the seed and the time you reap the harvest. A farmer does not plant seed and then dig it up the next day to see how it's doing.

Some Christians want to short-circuit God's law of sowing and reaping. They want to sow wild oats spiritually and then reap a harvest of wheat. They want to claim the promises of God without having to meet the conditions. They want to believe only portions of Scripture and ignore anything else that doesn't suit them.

I call these people Cafeteria Christians, because they pick what they like from Scripture and leave the rest alone. But it doesn't work that way. God's Word is one Word; it is not a spiritual smorgasbord.

These pick-and-choose Christians are like three little sisters who had just returned from a wedding. They decided to play their own game of wedding, and each child had a role to play: bride, groom, and minister. As the little bride and groom stood next to each other, the one playing the minister asked, "Do you take this man for richer or for poorer?" Without hesitation the make-believe bride replied, "For richer."

In the real world, it just doesn't work that way. You cannot pick and choose what portions of Scripture you want to believe or what commandments of God you will obey. You cannot receive God's promises without meeting His conditions.

Let me give you a couple of examples of conditional promises that are misused or misunderstood.

Look at Psalm 37:4–5:

> Delight yourself in the LORD
> and he will give you the desires of your heart.
> Commit your way to the LORD;
> trust in him and he will do this.

This is a conditional promise: If you delight yourself in the Lord and commit your way to Him, then He will give you the desires of your heart. But if you want to pilot your own ship your own way and then cry out to God to bail you out when you are in trouble, you have violated the condition of the promise and therefore the fulfillment of it.

Another conditional promise that is often misused is 1 John 1:9. This verse is often rattled off by carnal Christians, almost like dialing 9-1-1. They think that they can sin freely, then "dial" 1 John 1:9 for forgiveness. But what that verse says is this: "If we confess our sins, he is faithful and just and will forgive us our sins and purify us from all unrighteousness." It's conditional: If you confess, then He will forgive. You can't just live any way you please and then claim 1 John 1:9 for forgiveness.

Some people will claim they have confessed, when all they really did was mouth some words. Confession without the determination to change is cheap repentance and does not obligate God to forgive you. True confession must include the decision to forsake your sin.

Let me ask you this: What are you doing with the conditional promises of God? Are you refusing to keep the conditions, rationalizing that you don't really have to? Or have you simply given up, tired of waiting for God?

Do you want to be blessed financially? Examine your checkbook and see how much seed you have sown lately. Do you want to be blessed spiritually by having victory in a certain area in your life? Examine your calendar to see how much time you have spent in the Word and in prayer, specifically seeking that victory. Do you want your family to be blessed? Take a good look at your time spent with them for instruction, teaching, and praying.

God is true to His laws that He has set in motion, and when you meet the condition of the promise, He will fulfill it. Once you have met that condition, your job is to remain faithful in prayer until God intervenes. Trust that God will fulfill the promise—in due season.

The promises of God are certain, but they don't always mature in ninety days. I have often said that when God makes a promise, faith believes it, hope anticipates it, and patience quietly awaits it.

Now I am going to confess to you that when it comes to believing God's promise, I am okay with that. And when it comes to anticipating God's promise with hope, I can go along with that. But I have the hardest time with that last one, the patience that quietly awaits God's promise. You see, I have calluses on my hands from pounding on the doors of heaven!

But God's timing is not always our timing. Meet the conditions for God's promise, then trust Him—day by day—and He will fulfill it.

Elijah understood that whenever you align obedience to God with God's promises, God will answer. Whenever you fulfill the condition of the promise—this is true "naming-it-and-claiming-it"—you can safely claim the promise and it will be fulfilled.

Obedient Prayer

Elijah climbed to the top of Mount Carmel to kneel on the promises of God, while Ahab went down to eat and drink. Both men had just seen the power of God manifested in the greatest supernatural intervention since the Exodus. But one went off in a brutish, animalistic way to eat and drink, and the other went up in humility before God, clinging to His promises.

People often say that if we saw more miracles today, people would believe in God. They will not. I submit to you that there are miracles happening all around us all of the time, but the spiritually blind will not believe even when they see the most spectacular miracles.

Jesus told the story of a beggar named Lazarus and a rich man. (The story is found in Luke 16:19–31.) It is not a parable; it is a true story. Jesus Christ, who existed with the Father before the foundation of the world, related an actual event.

The man referred to as the rich man was self-centered. He had no thought of God or God's kingdom. He thought only of himself, his successes, his comfort.

The beggar, Lazarus, trusted God. He didn't have a thing in the world, but he believed God.

Both men died. One went to heaven and the other went to hell. Jesus said that when the rich man reached hell, he quickly turned into a fervent evangelist. After a few moments of torment he called out for "Father Abraham." He thought that his Jewishness would get him to heaven, so he called out to Abraham, the father of the Jewish nation. When the rich man finally realized that it was too late for him, he said, "Please send Lazarus to rise from the dead, for if my family sees him raised from the dead they will believe and not end up here in torment like me."

Abraham replied that if they will not believe Scripture, they will not be convinced even if someone rises from the dead.

King Ahab was just like the rich man in the story Jesus told. Miracles happened right before Ahab's eyes, but they did not pierce his heart. When you are engulfed in spiritual blindness, a miracle makes no difference.

Specific Prayer

There is something else here that I want you to note about Elijah's prayer. When Elijah went up to pray, he prayed specifically. Can you see his specific prayer in the text?

That was a trick question. There is no prayer recorded in the Old Testament account of this event. The Holy Spirit, who authored the Bible, did not record Elijah's prayer in 1 Kings 18. Instead, He recorded it some eight hundred years later in the book of James. "Elijah was a man just like us. He prayed earnestly that it would not rain, and it did not rain on the land for three and a half years. Again he prayed, and the heavens gave rain, and the earth produced its crops" (5:17–18).

What do you think Elijah was praying for on top of that mountain—"Oh, Lord, bless everybody everywhere"? I am convinced in my heart that he was praying, "Lord, You promised me that if I stood before Ahab it would rain. I obeyed Your command, and I believe You're going to fulfill Your promise now."

Do you know why prayer is such a burden to so many people? It is because of the ambiguity of our prayers. We look upon prayer as if it is a task. We feel the task is too heavy, so we end up with a "bless everyone everywhere" type of prayer.

Those who work closely with me know that I forget things on occasion. Someone will ask for my street address, and I have to call out to my wife or my secretary for the number of our house, because I am constantly confusing the addresses of our house and the church. What if I told that person: "Well, my home is at 3500 or 9500 or somewhere along there. I'm not sure, but just come anyway"?

You would quickly inform me that normal people don't give information to one another this way. That's true. And in that same sense, none of the great prayers in the Bible are ambiguous prayers. They are always prayers that came to God with specific requests.

Some people, out of a false sense of reverence, are afraid to be specific with God. Let me put an end to that fallacy. God has every single hair on your head numbered in chronological order. If God is that specific and detailed with you, then you need to be that specific and detailed with Him.

My wife and I have experienced the power of specific prayer many times. When we come together in total agreement, knowing that what we are praying for is the will of God and that it is consistent with Scripture, we have seen incredible answers to prayer. And when the answer comes, it is always bold, it is always clear, and it is very specific. I wish I could share some of these prayers with you, but because they affect other people, I am unable to give you the details. But I can assure you that God does answer specific prayers with specific answers.

Elijah obeyed God, and he prayed specifically. He also prayed persistently, clinging to the promises of God.

Persistent Prayer

This is the part that is the greatest challenge for me: persisting in prayer. Jesus often taught that it is not the length of prayer, it is not the language of prayer, it is not the posture of prayer, but it is persistence in prayer that He desires. I don't completely understand persistence in prayer, but in Scripture it is obvious that there is something about persistence that belongs together with God's promises. I am not talking about personal desires or wants; I am talking about persisting in prayer in order to receive God's promises.

Let's look at some examples of persistent prayer. In the Garden of Gethsemane, Jesus Himself persisted in prayer about the will of the Father (Matt. 26:36–46). The Syro-Phoenician woman, who came and sought Jesus on behalf of her daughter, would not take no for an answer. She stayed until He answered (Mark 7:24–30).

In Luke 18, Jesus told of the woman who pestered the ungodly judge and kept beating on his door. The judge finally grew tired of her persistence. "Even though I don't fear God," he said, "yet because this widow keeps bothering me, I will see that she gets justice" (vv. 4–5). The Bible makes it quite clear why Jesus told the disciples this woman's story: "to show them that they should always pray and not give up" (v. 1).

How did Elijah persist in prayer? Scripture says that while Elijah was praying on Mount Carmel, he sent his servant to look for clouds.

"There's nothing there," the servant said.

Elijah said, "Go back and look again."

The scene must have been almost comical as the servant went back and forth between Elijah and the sea, searching the skies for a sign of rain. Elijah kept sending him back until, on his seventh trip, the servant spotted a tiny cloud.

After the first time Elijah could have given up. He might have thought, *Maybe I didn't hear God right.* After the second time he could have said, "Looks like God is not going to answer me." After the third time he could have said, "I've had about enough victory for one day."

But he never doubted God, and he never got angry at God. He just kept looking for a cloud to appear. He was persistent in prayer. He sent his servant back a fourth time, and a fifth time, and a sixth time, even to the seventh time.

Elijah prayed obediently, specifically, persistently—and he also prayed expectantly. He believed with all of his heart that God would keep His word. Most of us are surprised when our prayers are answered, but Elijah would have been shocked if God had not answered. And that is why, 2,800 years later, we are still reading about Elijah.

We can tell how expectant Elijah was by his reaction when the servant finally spotted a tiny cloud "as small as a man's hand." At that moment Elijah started handing out umbrellas—that's expectancy in prayer. At the very first sign of a cloud, Elijah sent word to Ahab that he had better get his chariot moving unless he wanted to get drenched.

I want you to notice one last thing about Elijah's prayer. When God fulfilled His promise, when He sent rain in answer to Elijah's prayer, the prophet stayed humble before God. We see Elijah's humility in the fact that he tucked his cloak and ran ahead of the king's chariot. This was an act of submission and humility in Middle Eastern culture. To run before the king meant to subordinate yourself to him as a servant.

Elijah could have said, "Now I have Ahab exactly where I want him." But he didn't. He could have looked the king in the eye and said, "Ahab, I'm in and you're out." But he didn't. Why? Elijah was adamant that everybody know that this great act was God's act, not his own doing.

I have seen in the Christian community that some people do not know how to handle victory. They can handle a crisis, but somehow they can't handle blessings. I've seen others who, when victory comes, begin to take credit for it. "It was my hard work that accomplished this." Still others try to project human rationalism onto victory. "It would have happened anyway."

You don't have to be a great theologian to know that this kind of attitude is not honoring to God. Elijah, after this great victory, tucked his cloak and ran in humility before King Ahab.

Yet Elijah also shows us another problem that often travels with victory: depression and discouragement. A moment of great victory can be swiftly followed by great discouragement. Let's look now at how to handle this post-victory depression.

seven

Dealing with Depression and Discouragement

*T*he young man lay prostrate, completely incapacitated by the anguish of his soul. The birth of twin sons—his only children, it would turn out—should have been a joyous occasion. But a "horror of great darkness" had overtaken him the previous evening, October 19, 1856. Now, images of chaos flooded his mind and shouts of panic still rang in his ears. He would be haunted by the episode for years and would later say that he had come perilously near "the burning furnace of insanity."

The terrible accident happened at the young preacher's inaugural service at the grand Music Hall, the newest addition to the Royal Surrey Gardens. Just twenty-two years old, the "Boy Preacher of the Fens" (lowlands), had been pastor of New Park Street

Chapel in London for almost three years. Under his leadership the church had quickly outgrown the facilities. To accommodate the swelling crowds, the congregation rented a larger hall, then expanded their original building, which they promptly outgrew as well. When the new Music Hall opened, "with some trembling at the magnitude of the enterprise," the church booked it for Sunday evening services.

His tremendous success as a minister of the gospel had aroused considerable opposition. The London press had vilified the dynamic preacher, which only served to increase the number of souls—nobility and commoners alike—who thronged to hear him. In spite of the cruel caricatures and the ridiculous stories widely circulated, conversions continued to multiply.

At least seven thousand people filled the Music Hall that fateful evening in October. Among them were vicious critics who had come to create a disturbance. They waited until the singing had ceased and the pastor began to pray. Then several men shouted, "Fire!" and the crowd erupted in pandemonium. People began running frantically toward the exits, especially those sitting in the balconies. As they stampeded through the doors and down the stone staircase, some in the crowd were thrown down and trampled. Seven people died; twenty-eight were seriously injured.

Unaware of the critical injuries or the loss of life, the pastor stayed in the pulpit, trying to calm the crowd. His powerful voice carried above their screams, and many returned to their seats. But it was impossible to keep their attention, so he closed the service; the rest of the people left quietly.

When he discovered the extent of the calamity, the preacher succumbed to a terrible depression. He was unable to return to the pulpit, and his closest associates feared it signaled the end of a very promising ministry. Bitter accusations against him filled the newspapers, one report calling him a "ranting charlatan."

"I was pressed beyond measure," the pastor later wrote, "with an enormous weight of misery. The tumult, the panic, the deaths were day and night before me."

Yet, through the mercy of God, he was able to resume his ministry within a few weeks. He continued as pastor of the same congregation for another thirty-five years, until his death in 1892, and remains one of the most revered preachers of all time. He was also one of the most prolific: The complete collection of his printed sermons, which were transcribed by stenographers in his congregation, equals the length of the ninth edition of the *Encyclopedia Britannica*.[1]

A Necessary Heaviness of Heart

How did Charles Haddon Spurgeon, the "Prince of Preachers," recover from this crushing blow? Years later he told his students, "From that dream of horror I was awakened in a moment by the gracious application to my soul of the text, 'Him hath God the Father exalted.' The fact that Jesus is still great, let His servants suffer as they may, piloted me back to calm reason and peace."[2]

Recurring bouts of depression plagued Spurgeon throughout his ministry, however. Some of his battles with depression were due to extreme circumstances, such as the Music Hall catastrophe; some were due to poor health and painful physical afflictions (gout, rheumatism, kidney disease); and some were what he called "causeless depression"—a terrible sinking of the spirits without any apparent reason. "If those who laugh at such melancholy did but feel the grief of it for one hour," he said, "their laughter would be sobered into compassion."[3]

In a sermon preached at the Music Hall some two years after the disaster, Spurgeon told his listeners:

I was lying upon my couch during this last week, and my spirits were sunken so low that I could weep by the hour like a child, and yet I knew not what I wept for—but a very slight thing will move me to tears just now—and a kind friend was telling me of some poor old soul living near, who was suffering very great pain, and yet she was full of joy and rejoicing. I was so distressed by the hearing of that story, and felt so ashamed of myself, that I did not know what to do.[4]

As Spurgeon contemplated why he was in such a sorry state, for no reason he could determine, while the woman who was suffering painfully in the death throes of cancer was rejoicing, he thought of this verse: "Wherein ye greatly rejoice, though now for a season, if need be, ye are in heaviness through manifold temptations" (1 Peter 1:6 KJV). Then he understood that it is sometimes necessary for the Christian to experience such heaviness of heart, which he described in this way:

> your spirits are taken away from you; you are made to weep; you cannot bear your pain; you are brought to the very dust of death, and wish that you might die. Your faith itself seems as if it would fail you.[5]

Such "causeless depression" can be fruitful for those who minister, Spurgeon discovered. "You cannot help others who are depressed unless you have been down in the depths yourself."[6]

The "Common Cold of Mental Health Problems"

Have you ever found yourself, like the Prince of Preachers, in a state of emotional depression? You are certainly not alone! Consider these statistics about depression, often called the "common cold of mental health problems":

- More than 5 percent of Americans—some 15 million people—suffer clinical depression at any given moment.
- Another 5 percent experience mild symptoms of being "down in the dumps."
- At least one person in six experiences a serious, or "major," depressive episode at some point in life.
- Each year, tens of thousands of depressed people attempt suicide. About sixteen thousand succeed. Suicide is now a leading cause of death among teens and young adults.[7]

I am not a psychiatrist and I cannot explain things in medical terms, but I know enough from the Word of God and from pastoral experience to know the following. First, emotional depression is real. Second, there are different forms of depression. There is a depression that is psychological in origin, and there is a physical depression caused by chemical imbalances, which can be treated medically. In fact, deep emotional losses may trigger the biochemical changes that cause physical depression. When that happens, it affects the way nerve cells in the brain work.[8]

Here is the pattern I have noticed in dealing with emotional depression. It usually begins with self-protection, which occurs when you have been deeply hurt in some way. Someone may have failed you, or perhaps you feel that you have failed yourself. Your biggest dream has been demolished, your plans have collapsed, and all you are left with is a crushing disappointment.

At that point—if you have not been trained in your early years how to take your hurt to the Great Physician—you will pull into yourself and retreat from the realities of life. That is why we need to teach our children how to deal with life's disappointments rather than always trying to shelter them. They need to know where to go when they face such difficulties.

The Progression of Depression

When you are in the self-protection mode, you feel that you are safe only with yourself. You don't want to risk trusting others—they might hurt you again—so you withdraw. You retreat into your own little world.

The second step is self-pity. You begin to think that you are the only human being on the face of the earth who is hurting. "Nobody understands how I feel," you conclude. Of course, you feel so alone primarily because you have intentionally isolated yourself from everyone else. But that doesn't stop you from feeling sorry for yourself and lamenting your situation.

And that leads to the third step, which is self-punishment. You become judge and jury, condemning yourself to a life of self-inflicted pain. Why? To atone for whatever wrongs you imagine you have done. To punish your foolishness, which got you into this depressing state of affairs.

So this is the progression of depression: self-protection, self-pity, and self-punishment.

And when you reach this point, you will have an unwelcome visitor. He has been sitting there on the sidelines watching you, just waiting for an opportune moment. This enemy was the one whispering to you, "Nobody understands how you feel." He was the one saying, "You have really ruined your life, and you deserve every bit of this misery." When he finds you to be a receptive audience, he will attack in force.

Remember that Satan is the accuser of the brethren. He loves to remind you of your sins and mistakes. He delights in reminding you of past failures, even those embarrassing moments from fifty or sixty years ago that have already been covered by the blood of Jesus. And if you listen to Satan, each one of his reminders will make you feel worse and keep you sliding farther into depression.

As we turn back to the story of Elijah, who has just soared from victory to victory, we find him experiencing this very same progression into depression. Elijah had just run a fourteen-mile "Mount Carmel Marathon," in which he ran faster than the king's horses. He ran with a superhuman power—but the next thing you knew, he was running for his life. Afraid. Alone. Despairing of life itself.

---

1 Kings 19:1–18

Now Ahab told Jezebel everything Elijah had done and how he had killed all the prophets with the sword. So Jezebel sent a messenger to Elijah to say, "May the gods deal with me, be it ever so severely, if by this time tomorrow I do not make your life like that of one of them."

Elijah was afraid and ran for his life. When he came to Beersheba in Judah, he left his servant there, while he himself went a day's journey into the desert. He came to a broom tree, sat down under it and prayed that he might die. "I have had enough, LORD," he said. "Take my life; I am no better than my ancestors." Then he lay down under the tree and fell asleep.

All at once an angel touched him and said, "Get up and eat." He looked around, and there by his head was a cake of bread baked over hot coals, and a jar of water. He ate and drank and then lay down again.

The angel of the LORD came back a second time and touched him and said, "Get up and eat, for the journey is too much for you." So he got up and ate and drank. Strengthened by that food, he traveled forty days and forty nights until he reached Horeb, the mountain of God. There he went into a cave and spent the night.

And the word of the LORD came to him: "What are you doing here, Elijah?"

He replied, "I have been very zealous for the LORD God Almighty. The Israelites have rejected your covenant, broken down your altars, and put your prophets to death with the sword. I am the only one left, and now they are trying to kill me too."

The LORD said, "Go out and stand on the mountain in the presence of the LORD, for the LORD is about to pass by."

Then a great and powerful wind tore the mountains apart and shattered the rocks before the LORD, but the LORD was not in the wind. After the wind there was an earthquake, but the LORD was not in the earthquake. After the earthquake came a fire, but the LORD was not in the fire. And after the fire came a gentle whisper. When Elijah heard it, he pulled his cloak over his face and went out and stood at the mouth of the cave.

Then a voice said to him, "What are you doing here, Elijah?"

He replied, "I have been very zealous for the

LORD God Almighty. The Israelites have rejected your covenant, broken down your altars, and put your prophets to death with the sword. I am the only one left, and now they are trying to kill me too."

The LORD said to him, "Go back the way you came, and go to the Desert of Damascus. When you get there, anoint Hazael king over Aram. Also, anoint Jehu son of Nimshi king over Israel, and anoint Elisha son of Shaphat from Abel Meholah to succeed you as prophet. Jehu will put to death any who escape the sword of Hazael, and Elisha will put to death any who escape the sword of Jehu. Yet I reserve seven thousand in Israel—all whose knees have not bowed down to Baal and all whose mouths have not kissed him."

"Just Kill Me, Lord"

When Elijah arrived at Beersheba, about one hundred miles south of Carmel, he left his servant behind and went on, traveling a day's journey into the desert. There he collapsed under a juniper tree, put his head between his knees, and said, "God, just go ahead and kill me. I've had enough."

What had Elijah been doing just before this? He had called down fire from heaven, he had successfully prayed for rain to end a drought of three and a half years, and he had outrun the king's chariot. But what happened next is a textbook case in spiritual warfare: At the very moment of great victory, the enemy will viciously attack the servant of God.

Let's see how the enemy's assault unfolded against Elijah.

King Ahab had witnessed the fire from heaven. He had watched Elijah run faster than his royal stallions. And he knew that Elijah's prayer was responsible for ending the drought. Yet he still was not repentant of his spiritual compromise, of having allowed the people of Israel to confuse Yahweh with Baal. And Ahab not only was a compromiser, he was a coward.

So as Ahab returned to the palace, all he could think about was, *What am I going to tell Jezebel? How am I going to explain Mount Carmel?* I imagine his face was so downcast that he walked in with his lip dragging the ground. And his domineering, controlling, nature-worshiping wife was waiting for him. She probably wound her fingers around his ears and said, "What's wrong, big boy?"

I think Ahab had a child-mother relationship instead of a husband-wife relationship with Jezebel. He was overdependent on her. He let her take complete control of the life of the kingdom. She was in charge of the decision-making process.

When Ahab told Jezebel what happened, he never once mentioned God's mighty hand. He never said, "Jezebel, Yahweh is the Lord and I am going to trust only in Him." He could have told her that Elijah got rid of the prophets of Baal and that he would finish the job and remove Baal from the royal household. But he didn't.

The moment wicked Jezebel heard what happened to her precious prophets of Baal, she became enraged. I can picture her lips quivering and her hands shaking as she swore by her gods—who had turned out to be useless—that she would put a contract on Elijah's life. She immediately sent word to the prophet that she had hired a hit man, and she promised Elijah that he would be history in twenty-four hours.

And Elijah, fresh from calling down fire and praying down rain, fell victim to fear. His boldness, his persistence, his unwavering trust in God, all evaporated.

Let me tell you that this is exactly what happens when you get a great victory from the hand of the Lord. Satan becomes furious, so he immediately uses someone—a family member, a friend, or even a fellow Christian—to steal away the joy of your victory. And the thing that poisons your joy will always be a minor thing in comparison to the great victory that God has given you.

The Bible says that when he heard from Jezebel, "Elijah was afraid" (1 Kings 19:3). He had not been afraid when he confronted Ahab. He had not been afraid on Mount Carmel in front of 850 pagan prophets. He had not been afraid in Zarephath, the very heart of the Baal-worshiping gentile world. But now, suddenly, he was afraid of Jezebel.

So he ran for his life. And out in the desert, where it was 130 degrees in the shade, he cried out to God. "Okay, Lord, I've had enough. Just go ahead and kill me now."

Elijah was not the only great man who ever said something like that to God. Other biblical all-stars became despondent or suicidal after great victories.

Moses, for example, saw the Red Sea part, led more than a million people across on dry land, and then watched Pharaoh and his army drown as the waters reformed and crashed down on them. But later, exasperated by his people's murmuring and complaining and criticizing, Moses told God, "If this is how you are going to treat me, put me to death right now" (Num. 11:15).

Jonah was rescued from being fish food so he could preach in Nineveh, where he had a great victory. But he was angry with God for sending him there, and angry that God spared the wicked Ninevites when they turned to Him. So Jonah said, "O LORD, take away my life, for it is better for me to die than to live" (Jonah 4:3).

Jeremiah, the weeping prophet, became so wearied with the people's indifference to God and God's work that he despaired of his life. "Why did I ever come out of the womb . . . ?" he complained (Jer. 20:18).

If you have never been in such a place, take note, because sooner or later you may enter the realm of despair.

Don't Move Without a Word from God

Let me give you some lessons that can keep you from those moments of despondency, or at least shorten their duration. First, never proceed without a word from the Lord. Never respond to the enemy's post-victory assault without hearing from God first.

When we study the scriptural account of Elijah's life, we see that he was a man whose movements and messages were ordered by God. Notice these examples.

"Then the word of the LORD came to Elijah: 'Leave here, turn eastward and hide in the Kerith Ravine'" (1 Kings 17:2). After Elijah's initial confrontation with Ahab, the prophet received God's word to leave. God's word was explicit, telling Elijah exactly where to hide.

"Then the word of the LORD came to him: 'Go at once to Zarephath of Sidon and stay there'" (1 Kings 17:8–9). At God's word, Elijah left the brook in the wilderness and went to Zarephath to live with the widow and her son. And he stayed put until he received further instruction from the Lord.

"After a long time, in the third year, the word of the LORD came to Elijah: 'Go and present yourself to Ahab, and I will send rain on the land'" (1 Kings 18:1).

But what did Elijah do when Jezebel threatened his life? What is missing from the biblical account of that occasion ought to hit you between the eyes: There was no word from the Lord. Elijah did not wait to hear from God, he simply ran in fear. When he was in danger before, God had directed him to a hiding place. When the brook had dried up, God sent him to another place of provision. When Jezebel sought to kill him, God had a plan to protect His prophet, but Elijah did not wait to hear a word from the Lord.

To put it bluntly, Elijah got blindsided. His example reminds us that the best of men are only men at best.

Have you ever been blindsided? Perhaps you received a letter or a phone call you were not expecting, a confrontation you would rather not have received. Wait for a word from the Lord! Do not respond immediately; you may not need to respond at all.

If you want to avoid despondency and depression, the first lesson is this: Do not make a major decision without a word from the Lord, particularly if you have just experienced a great spiritual victory.

The second principle is this: Do not isolate yourself when you reach a low point.

Do Not Isolate Yourself

Elijah wanted to be left alone at the time when he most needed someone. He made his servant stay at Beersheba while he continued into the desert by himself. There he sat under the tree and asked God to take his life.

When you move from great victory to sudden defeat, this is not the time to be alone. There are times when you must surely be alone with God in prayer; this is vitally important. But be careful about withdrawing from people. Don't start down the progression to depression.

Imagine for a moment what might have happened if Elijah had not left his servant at Beersheba. According to tradition, this servant was the son of the widow in Zarephath, the young man raised from the dead. If the servant was indeed the widow's son, what might he have said to Elijah when he overheard the prophet asking God to kill him? He would have said, "Oh, no, Elijah! Don't you remember what God did for us in Zarephath? Don't you remember how the oil and the flour were multiplied? Don't you remember that I was dead, and you stretched yourself out over me, and God brought me to life again? Don't despair; there is hope in God.

"Have you forgotten the fire from heaven that consumed everything in sight, including the water? And don't you remember how you sent me out toward the sea to look for rain? Seven times you sent me back, and you never doubted God. God answered your prayer and the rain came. Elijah, God is still in the miracle-working business!"

Like Elijah, you do not need to be alone at the low point of your life. This is one purpose for being active in a church, and especially a small group or Bible study: mutual fellowship, encouragement, and upholding the Word of God. We are members of one body, designed to work together. We need one another.

If you are trying to walk alone, that is the last thing you should be doing. Let God give you a Christian friend to walk with through the rough spots of life.

Don't Lose Your Perspective

Another principle I want you to see in this passage is that when you are down, you lose perspective. You lose objectivity about the circumstances and about God's sovereignty.

Did you notice the paradox in our text? Scripture says that Elijah ran away from Jezebel because he didn't want her to kill him. But then he goes to God and says, "Kill me." What is this double-talk? If Elijah wanted to die, all he had to do was stay put. Jezebel would have killed him with a passion.

But when you are in the depths of despair and defeat, you lose touch with reality.

Look at something else Elijah said: "I am no better than my ancestors." What does that mean?

Elijah began to think of the thousands of people who had lived faithfully for Yahweh, who had died for Yahweh—those nameless people throughout the generations, all the way back to Moses. He thought, *I'm no better than they are. What good did it do them to serve God? I might as well die right now.*

The next time you sit down and have a personal pity party, remember Elijah under the juniper tree. There he sat, spiraling down the progression of depression. He had gone from self-protection to self-pity and then self-punishment. "Why don't You just kill me, God, and get it over with?" Suicidal thoughts—the ultimate self-punishment.

The Exhaustion of Depression

The bottom line of Elijah's depression is this: exhaustion. Elijah was exhausted physically, emotionally, and spiritually.

As soon as he had prayed to die, Scripture says, he lay down under the tree and fell asleep. It was the sleep of depression.

Depression always causes a sleep disturbance, either wide-eyed insomnia or excessive sleeping. Elijah fell into a despondent and depleting sleep, that sleep from which you wake up more tired than when you went to bed. When you allow yourself to become as totally exhausted as Elijah, sleep will not refresh you, even if you stay in bed for twenty-four hours.

I have experienced this kind of exhaustion first-hand. As I related earlier, I escaped from my country of birth by the skin of my teeth—and the grace of God. In the years that followed, a new regime came to power, and the political atmosphere became much more relaxed. In 1977, nine years after I had left home, I received an invitation to return to Egypt. The invitation came from President Anwar Sadat, who requested that I visit him personally.

Thrilled by the honor of this invitation, I began to make my travel plans. But as the initial excitement wore off and the day of departure drew closer, an absurd and irrational fear gripped me. The two nights before I left, I slept for less than an hour. During the three nights I was in Egypt, I slept even less.

As I tossed and turned in bed, my mind played and replayed a series of torturous "what-if" questions. *What if the invitation were merely a ruse to get me in the country, so I could be punished for leaving?* I recalled the general's angry diatribe against Christians, how he had told me he "knew what to do with troublemakers." *What if I were thrown in jail while I was there? What would happen to my family?*

Periodically I got out of bed and turned on the light. I would read my official letter of invitation, trying to regain a semblance of peace. *God is in control. Everything will work out,* I told myself. Yet as soon as I climbed back into bed, the questions would start again. *But what if . . .*

After five nights with a grand total of five hours of sleep, I was exhausted beyond belief. As soon as I went through customs and immigration and was actually at the gate where my flight to India would depart, I fell into a deep sleep. I slept for almost forty-eight hours straight, waking up just long enough to board and disembark the plane and get to my hotel.

So I empathize with Elijah as I read in Scripture that he fell into the sleep of depression under the juniper tree.

Why was Elijah so exhausted? He was physically exhausted because he had just run a hundred miles to get away from Jezebel. And nothing can exhaust you emotionally and spiritually like spiritual warfare. You do not endure the confrontation with the prophets of Baal on Mount Carmel, then spend time imploring God to fulfill His promises, and then confront the most wicked woman in the kingdom, without being emotionally and spiritually depleted.

This is an important concept you need to remember: *Ministry takes life out of you.* If you want to do great things for God without reaching the depths of depression and discouragement, then you must not allow yourself to become physically, emotionally, and spiritually exhausted.

But if, like Elijah, you do get to that point of incapacitating exhaustion, here is the best part of the story: God will restore you in compassion and tenderness.

God's Compassion for Depression

To me the greatest part about this episode in Elijah's life is not his depression or discouragement. It is not his weakness or fear. No, the greatest part of this story is how God restored him. This is the nugget of nuggets in the nineteenth chapter of 1 Kings.

The Bible does not say, "And the Lord God yelled at Elijah and said to him, 'You weak-willed, vacillating wimp. I gave you an important assignment and you blew it.'" Never, never, never!

How does God deal with a depressed and discouraged servant? This is very important, especially for all of you superachievers and perfectionists. You are harder on yourselves than God is. Quit trying to be a super-Christian!

Look at God's kindness to Elijah. When Elijah was in despair, God matched his every need at every point.

Even though Elijah had not waited for a word from the Lord, the Lord gave him a word anyway.

Even though Elijah had refused a human companion, God sent an angel to minister to him.

Because he needed food and refreshment, God supernaturally provided it.

God met Elijah at every point of his need.

When you are depressed or discouraged, God does not say, "You imbecile, you have failed. You have let Me down." That is not how God deals with His faithful children when they get blindsided by the enemy.

God knew that Elijah needed some R and R more than anything else. The angel did not say to him, "Elijah, get up and ponder the great doctrine of the sovereignty of God." At that point in his life, Elijah needed food and drink, not doctrine. He did not need a book to read or a cassette tape to listen to. There is a place and a time for that, but what Elijah needed at that moment was to eat and drink and to rest. After he ate and drank, he went back to sleep. His body was in desperate need of sleep.

After he had rested, the angel woke him up. Now Elijah was ready to resume his ministry. God was ready to talk to him. And note that God did not speak to His prophet through the earthquake or the fire. God spoke to him in a gentle whisper. It was time for God to set him straight, to correct his wrong thinking that had set him on the spiral into depression. But He corrected His servant in gentleness and compassion.

And He will deal with you in the same manner. He is

"the Father of compassion and the God of all comfort" (2 Cor. 1:3).

God's Sovereignty over Depression

Like Elijah, Charles Spurgeon often heard the gentle whisper of God as he lay on a bed of affliction. This Prince of Preachers came to understand his recurring depression in the context of the sovereignty of God.

Spurgeon realized that his sovereign Lord had allowed him to suffer such heaviness of heart and despair of the soul for a purpose, and that purpose had to do with the gifts and calling of God on his life. He knew that God could and would lift him out of a deep depression in a moment's time, but he learned to endure his melancholy patiently. He became long-suffering, so that God could work out His purposes in His timing.

This great preacher also shared what he had learned with his students, to help them understand how unexplained suffering plays a part in the Christian's, and especially the minister's, life. Over one hundred years later Spurgeon's words are still a blessing to those who are physically, emotionally, and spiritually exhausted by the battle.

Knowing by most painful experience what deep depression of spirit means, being visited therewith at seasons by no means few or far between,

I thought it might be consolatory to some of my brethren if I gave my thoughts thereon, that younger men might not fancy that some strange thing had happened to them when they became for a season possessed by melancholy . . .

These infirmities may be no detriment to a man's career of special usefulness; they may even have been imposed upon him by divine wisdom as necessary qualifications for his peculiar course of service . . . Grace has its triumphs still, and patience has its martyrs; martyrs none the less to be honoured because the flames kindle about their spirits rather than their bodies, and their burning is unseen of human eyes . . . "Blessed are they that mourn," said the Man of Sorrows, and let none account them otherwise when their tears are salted with grace.[9]

What a comfort it is to know that it is not at all unusual for the believer to be depressed or discouraged. Bible heroes and spiritual leaders throughout church history have waged the same struggles. Take heart that you are not alone; others have walked this path before you. Allow God to work out His purposes in you, even when you are at your lowest point. He will restore you in gentleness and compassion.

Learn to trust God's sovereign purposes even when you do not understand His ways. Let's turn now to a thorny problem that has caused many believers to stumble: why the innocent often suffer.

eight

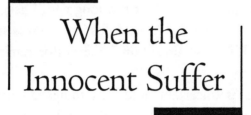

When the Innocent Suffer

Five identical coffins lined the front of the church as Pastor Max Johnson presided over the first of a series of funerals for the devastated community of Jarrell, Texas. Music was the focus of the service, but First Baptist's music director, Larry Igo, was not there to lead the congregation in a hymn. His remains were in the first coffin; the other four belonged to Larry's wife, Joan, their seventeen-year-old daughter, Audrey, and fifteen-year-old twin sons, John and Paul.

Four days earlier a force F-5 tornado, one of the deadliest storms on record, had cut a half-mile-wide swath through tiny Jarrell, population four hundred. The gigantic funnel of wind, which stayed on the ground for six miles, sucked the asphalt off roads and blasted fifty homes into matchstick-size pieces. Twenty-seven people lost their lives, including all five members of the Igo family.

At the funeral Pastor Johnson recalled Joan's beautiful singing voice. "Not too long ago, I asked her to sing at my funeral," he said. Instead, he was singing at hers. "Life is so uncertain," the pastor reminded the mourners.[1]

Life *is* uncertain, and bad things do happen to good people. One of the bad things that can hurt good people is a natural disaster, like the Jarrell tornado, which does not discriminate between the innocent and the guilty. Nature's bountiful blessing and its destructive power fall on everyone equally. Scripture says that God causes the "sun to rise on the evil and the good, and sends rain on the righteous and the unrighteous" (Matt. 5:45).

But the righteous often suffer at the hands of the unrighteous. And that messes up some people's theology.

An unscrupulous man wreaks financial havoc on the owner of a small business, forcing a godly family to struggle through bankruptcy and deprivation. A drunk driver mows down innocent children playing in their own front yard. A stray bullet from a gang shooting kills a bystander who just happened to be in the wrong place at the wrong time. A Christian woman is kidnapped, raped, and killed; her family suffers such a devastating loss that they are never quite the same.

If God is in control of all of creation, why does He allow terrible things to happen to His people? Can being raped and murdered really be a part of His plan for a godly woman's life? How do we understand God's sovereignty when the innocent suffer?

Before we return to our Scripture study, let's look at a couple of examples from more recent history. I've already shared with you the story of how wicked men shouted "fire" in a crowded auditorium and church people were killed and injured in the resulting stampede. Charles Spurgeon was well acquainted with grief and suffering. Yet he viewed all his suffering as being filtered through God's hands.

> It would be a very sharp and trying experience to me to think that I have an affliction which God never sent me, that the bitter cup was never filled by his hand, that my trials were never measured out by him, not sent to me by his arrangement of their weight and quantity . . .
>
> As long as I trace my pain to accident, my bereavement to mistake, my loss to another's wrong, my discomfort to an enemy, and so on, I am of the earth, earthy, and shall break my teeth with gravel stones; but when I rise to my God and

see his hand at work, I grow calm, I have not a word of repining.[2]

Spurgeon's steadfast faith in God's loving sovereignty did not keep him from questioning God or asking why some things happened. But he never doubted that an infinite God could make sense out of the incomprehensible, and that He would indeed work "all things . . . together for good" (Rom. 8:28 KJV).

Another example of unwavering trust in God's sovereignty comes from World War II. A Christian family in Holland was sent to prison for the crime of hiding Jews in their home, in an effort to keep them from being slaughtered in Hitler's Holocaust. As Betsie ten Boom lay dying in a Nazi concentration camp, she spoke to her sister Corrie of how the Lord would use their experiences. "We must tell people what we have learned here. We must tell them that there is no pit so deep that He is not deeper still. They will listen to us, Corrie, because we have been here."[3]

There is no pit so deep . . . These were not the pat words of a wet-behind-the-ears believer mouthing untried promises. These were the final words of a frail woman ravaged by the horror of existence in a hellhole named Ravensbruck. Betsie did not live to give her testimony of God's loving provision for the brutalized, starving, flea-infested prisoners of Barracks 28. But

Corrie ten Boom spent the next forty years doing exactly what Betsie had seen by faith: telling a jaded world that God's love was far greater than any torture man could devise. She knew. She had been there.

We must learn to live with the fact that evil exists in this fallen world and will until the end of time. God has ordained that here on earth. Life is not fair. Sometimes, in fact, it is very cruel. But there will be a day, in the fullness of time, when life *will* be fair, when the righteous will be rewarded and the wicked will be punished.

God will have the last word. He will hold evildoers accountable. That is why Psalm 37 says, "Do not fret because of evil men" (v. 1). "The Lord laughs at the wicked," according to verse 13, "for he knows their day is coming."

A King's Greed

Elijah understood that God would have the last word when it came to the wicked rulers of Israel, Ahab and Jezebel. In the Scripture passage we will examine next, we find that an innocent man is suffering because of the evil king and queen.

It was a classic case of unbridled greed. The fever of wanting more and more can only produce perpetual pain and emptiness, and in this instance it led to theft by fraud and murder.

1 Kings 21:1–28

Some time later there was an incident involving a vineyard belonging to Naboth the Jezreelite. The vineyard was in Jezreel, close to the palace of Ahab king of Samaria. Ahab said to Naboth, "Let me have your vineyard to use for a vegetable garden, since it is close to my palace. In exchange I will give you a better vineyard or, if you prefer, I will pay you whatever it is worth."

But Naboth replied, "The LORD forbid that I should give you the inheritance of my fathers."

So Ahab went home, sullen and angry because Naboth the Jezreelite had said, "I will not give you the inheritance of my fathers." He lay on his bed sulking and refused to eat.

His wife Jezebel came in and asked him, "Why are you so sullen? Why won't you eat?"

He answered her, "Because I said to Naboth the Jezreelite, 'Sell me your vineyard; or if you prefer, I will give you another vineyard in its place.' But he said, 'I will not give you my vineyard.'"

Jezebel his wife said, "Is this how you act as king over Israel? Get up and eat! Cheer up. I'll get you the vineyard of Naboth the Jezreelite."

So she wrote letters in Ahab's name, placed his seal on them, and sent them to the elders and nobles who lived in Naboth's city with him. In those letters she wrote:

"Proclaim a day of fasting and seat Naboth in a prominent place among the people. But seat two scoundrels opposite him and have them testify that he has cursed both God and the king. Then take him out and stone him to death."

So the elders and nobles who lived in Naboth's city did as Jezebel directed in the letters she had written to them. They proclaimed a fast and seated Naboth in a prominent place among the people. Then two scoundrels came and sat opposite him and brought charges against Naboth before the people, saying, "Naboth has cursed both God and the king." So they took him outside the city and stoned him to death. Then they sent word to Jezebel: "Naboth has been stoned and is dead."

As soon as Jezebel heard that Naboth had been stoned to death, she said to Ahab, "Get up and take possession of the vineyard of Naboth the Jezreelite that he refused to sell you. He is no longer alive, but dead." When Ahab heard that

Naboth was dead, he got up and went down to take possession of Naboth's vineyard.

Then the word of the LORD came to Elijah the Tishbite: "Go down to meet Ahab king of Israel, who rules in Samaria. He is now in Naboth's vineyard, where he has gone to take possession of it. Say to him, 'This is what the LORD says: Have you not murdered a man and seized his property?' Then say to him, 'This is what the LORD says: In the place where dogs licked up Naboth's blood, dogs will lick up your blood—yes, yours!'"

Ahab said to Elijah, "So you have found me, my enemy!"

"I have found you," he answered, "because you have sold yourself to do evil in the eyes of the LORD. 'I am going to bring disaster on you. I will consume your descendants and cut off from Ahab every last male in Israel—slave or free. I will make your house like that of Jeroboam son of Nebat and that of Baasha son of Ahijah, because you have provoked me to anger and have caused Israel to sin.'

"And also concerning Jezebel the LORD says: 'Dogs will devour Jezebel by the wall of Jezreel.'

"Dogs will eat those belonging to Ahab who die in the city, and the birds of the air will feed on those who die in the country."

(There was never a man like Ahab, who sold himself to do evil in the eyes of the LORD, urged on by Jezebel his wife. He behaved in the vilest manner by going after idols, like the Amorites the LORD drove out before Israel.)

When Ahab heard these words, he tore his clothes, put on sackcloth and fasted. He lay in sackcloth and went around meekly.

Then the word of the LORD came to Elijah the Tishbite: "Have you noticed how Ahab has humbled himself before me? Because he has humbled himself, I will not bring this disaster in his day, but I will bring it on his house in the days of his son."

A poor, simple, but faithful man by the name of Naboth owned a small vineyard that butted up against the garden of the king's summer palace in Jezreel. The vineyard was Naboth's inheritance, and he refused to sell it to Ahab when the king's greed determined that he should expand his garden and swallow up the vineyard.

There was a certain psychology of what it meant for a Jewish man to own a vineyard as his inheritance. A vineyard was the very emblem of Israel itself, a sign of fruitfulness. In Isaiah 5, God compared Israel to a vineyard. So to own a vineyard was to possess the heart of Israel.

But poor Naboth! His inheritance from his ancestors happened to be next to the royal garden. King Ahab felt incomplete without owning all of the surrounding land.

No matter how much a greedy person has, he feels incomplete. So he tries to get more. More does not make him complete, of course, so he strives to get still more. But he never feels complete at all. He never reaches the place of the apostle Paul, who had "learned to be content whatever the circumstances" (Phil. 4:11).

A tombstone in a cemetery outside of London sums up the futility of greed. It reads, "She died for want of things." Alongside that stone is another that reads, "He died trying to give them to her."

Greed was once characterized as one of the seven deadly sins. In days gone by, the word *greed* conjured up images of a miserly Ebenezer Scrooge in the back room counting and recounting his money. But now, thanks to Hollywood, greed has become much more benign and attractive. In 1987 Michael Douglas earned an Oscar for his portrayal of a financial tycoon in Oliver Stone's *Wall Street.* On the big screen Douglas convincingly uttered this memorable line: "Greed is good."

No, greed is not good. It is as old as the Garden of Eden and as modern as Imelda Marcos's shoe closet, but it is not good. And greed is often misunderstood. Let me give you a biblical definition of greed.

The Communists consider private ownership, hard work, and the accumulation of property or goods to be the evil greed of Western capitalism. That is not biblical greed.

Liberal politicians often say that it is greed when working people are not willing to toss all their earnings into the big money furnace known as the IRS, to be redistributed among those who can work but won't. That is not biblical greed.

Simply put, biblical greed is when you look at the one thing God says you cannot have, and you reach out to get it. God told Adam and Eve they could eat from any tree in the garden, except one. That one tree became the object of their greed.

Greed is an obsession with getting what you do not have. It is being discontented no matter what you have or don't have. It is a constant inner emptiness. Greed is getting in your car and going to the mall to buy something you don't need and will probably never use. This is the proper definition of greed.

There is a fine line between greed and the breaking of the law to fulfill the desire of your greed.

A Greed That Murdered

Ahab had enough knowledge of the law of God that he would not cross that line, but not Jezebel, the Baal worshiper. She was eager to cross the line to fulfill Ahab's greed.

When Naboth refused to sell his vineyard, Ahab sulked. Not Jezebel. She went into action. "Get up, eat and drink," she said. "I will kill to give you what your heart covets."

Jezebel was a woman of determination, which compensated for the weak-willed Ahab. While the king still had a few moral compunctions, which came from his Jewish heritage, Jezebel had none. She never let anyone or anything stand in her way. Scripture shows how her obsessive determination led to forgery, hypocrisy, and treachery.

First, Jezebel forged a letter in the king's name. Then she stole his signet ring to stamp his name on the letter. When the media confronted her, she said she was only helping the king do the job he was elected to do. She was the kind of woman who would lie under oath, and everyone thought she was charming and convincing.

Look at the hypocrisy. She told the population of Jezreel to proclaim a day of fasting. Her public relations staff must have explained to her that when the Jewish people wanted to announce a coming judgment, the king would announce a day of fasting. So that's what she did. She wasn't the king, but she functioned as one, even if she had to forge his name to do it.

Next, she bribed two false witnesses to testify against this faithful man of God, Naboth. He was one of the seven thousand righteous Israelites who had not bowed down to Baal. Jezebel used the law of God to do her dirty work. She called for a day of fasting and then brought two false witnesses to say publicly that Naboth had blasphemed God and the king, and that he therefore deserved capital punishment, which meant being stoned to death.

You can almost picture the astonishment, the terror, the icy fear that gripped Naboth when he heard these false accusations. Imagine the gnawing in the pit of his stomach as he realized what was about to happen. I can see Naboth covering his eyes as his accusers began to reach for stones to kill him—in the name of God.

Do you know that the very same thing is happening around the world today? In Muslim countries it is common to bring two witnesses to falsely accuse a Christian of blaspheming against Islam or Allah or Muhammad. Many are executed and others are imprisoned for life for their supposed crimes.

In Pakistan, a Muslim cleric accused twelve-year-old Salamat Masih and two other Christians of writing blasphemies against Muhammad on the walls of a mosque. The slogans were so bad, he claimed, that he immediately washed them off the walls. The cleric also refused to repeat the offensive words for the court. There was no other evidence presented at the trial. Nevertheless, the three were convicted of blasphemy, a capital offense in Pakistan. Because of international pressure the conviction was overturned before they could be executed, but one defendant was murdered by extremists and the other two fled the country. Now a teenager, Salamat lives in exile, with a price on his head.[4]

This is the kind of flimsy case Jezebel mounted against Naboth. Manufactured evidence from false witnesses. A godly man framed for a crime he didn't commit.

Where Was God?

Scripture says that when Jezebel heard Naboth had been killed, she went to Ahab and said, "The vineyard is yours for the taking." She probably delighted in telling Ahab that he could now have the vineyard because Naboth was dead. "It's my gift to you, darling." And with a cold, calloused heart Ahab went and took possession of an innocent man's inheritance.

There is a question every honest person asks at some point in life. Great men and women in the Bible have asked the same question: *Where is God?*

Where was God when an honest man like Naboth was murdered? Where was God when a wicked woman like Jezebel defiled a whole nation? Where was God when a coward like Ahab went into Naboth's vineyard to enjoy the fruit of his greed? Where was God in all of this?

This is the question the psalmist asked in Psalm 73. In fact, he confesses that he nearly slipped—he nearly lost his spiritual foothold—when he began to ask that question: Where is God? It looked as if the wicked were getting away with their wickedness. "They wear pride like a necklace," he wrote, "and clothe themselves with violence"(v. 6). And they got away with it. Or so it seemed.

Like the psalmist, we must come to the understanding that God *is* there. The fact that He is merciful and long-suffering does not mean that He is not just. Do not judge by appearances. And do not think that this life is all there is. The goodness of God will be made manifest, and He will bring justice on the wicked.

My flesh and my heart may fail,
　but God is the strength of my heart
　and my portion forever.
Those who are far from you will perish;
　you destroy all who are unfaithful to you.
But as for me, it is good to be near God.
　I have made the Sovereign LORD
　my refuge. (Ps. 73:26–28)

God Will Have the Last Word

Let's return to 1 Kings 21 to see how God always has the last word. God instructed Elijah to go down to the vineyard and confront Ahab. Where was God when an innocent man suffered? He was right there. He saw that the wicked king was now enjoying the fruit of his sin in Naboth's vineyard.

God even told Elijah what to say to Ahab: "'This is what the LORD says: Have you not murdered a man and seized his property?' Then say to him, 'This is what the LORD says: In the place where dogs licked up Naboth's blood, dogs will lick up your blood—yes, yours!'" (v. 19).

The message of God for Ahab was that there will be consequences for every wicked act. In this particular instance, God simply sped up the process so we could see His justice. Elijah delivered God's word to the guilty party. "Don't enjoy your vineyard too much, Ahab, because you will pay for it dearly. The dogs that licked Naboth's blood will soon lick yours." I imagine the king felt a twinge of remorse every time he heard a dog bark after that. Scripture implies that he felt remorse— he tore his clothes (a sign of grief or mourning) and fasted—but there is no evidence that Ahab ever truly repented.

What is the lesson for us? Never construe God's patience as indifference or unfairness. God does not mete out justice according to our timetable, and He rarely executes judgment immediately.

It was an exception that God confronted Adam in

the Garden (Gen. 3:8–9). It was an exception that Nathan confronted David with his sin (2 Sam. 12:1–14). It was an exception that Ananias and Sapphira dropped dead immediately after lying to the apostles (Acts 5:1–10).

These may be exceptions, but they are examples. And these scriptural examples remind us that the consequences of sin can be immediate or delayed, but they are inevitable. Make no mistake about it: No one will escape the justice of God. God will always have the last word.

The demise of Ahab and Jezebel dramatically illustrates that God always has the last word. Elijah prophesied God's judgment against the wicked king and queen. He not only declared that dogs would lick Ahab's blood, he said that "dogs will devour Jezebel by the wall of Jezreel" (1 Kings 21:23). God's judgment was fulfilled to the letter.

About three years later, Ahab and Jehoshaphat, king of Judah, went to war with the king of Aram. Another prophet, Micaiah, had prophesied that the Lord was luring Ahab to his death through the battle. Even though the prophet said he would not survive, Ahab went ahead with his war plans. To fool his enemy, who had vowed to destroy the king of Israel, Ahab wore a disguise into battle. Perhaps Ahab thought he could outwit God as well as the Arameans.

1 Kings 22:29–38

So the king of Israel and Jehoshaphat king of Judah went up to Ramoth Gilead. The king of Israel said to Jehoshaphat, "I will enter the battle in disguise, but you wear your royal robes." So the king of Israel disguised himself and went into battle.

Now the king of Aram had ordered his thirty-two chariot commanders, "Do not fight with anyone, small or great, except the king of Israel." When the chariot commanders saw Jehoshaphat, they thought, "Surely this is the king of Israel." So they turned to attack him, but when Jehoshaphat cried out, the chariot commanders saw that he was not the king of Israel and stopped pursuing him.

But someone drew his bow at random and hit the king of Israel between the sections of his armor. The king told his chariot driver, "Wheel around and get me out of the fighting. I've been wounded." All day long the battle raged, and the king was propped up in his chariot facing the Arameans. The blood from his wound ran onto the floor of the chariot, and that evening he died. As the sun was setting, a cry spread through the army: "Every man to his town; everyone to his land!"

So the king died and was brought to Samaria, and they buried him there. They washed the chariot at a pool in Samaria (where the prostitutes bathed), and the dogs licked up his blood, as the word of the LORD had declared.

Ahab was shot during the battle. Different Bible translations use various words to describe the arrow that struck Ahab, but they all imply that it was an arbitrary thing, a random shot that just happened to hit the king between the sections of his armor. There are no accidents with God, however. God had ordained an arrow with Ahab's name on it. That arrow found its target, in spite of Ahab's disguise.

King Ahab told his chariot driver to get him out of the fighting, because he was wounded. The battle continued throughout the day, while Ahab, out of the line of fire, remained propped up in his chariot, watching helplessly, his blood running onto the floor of the chariot. After they buried him, Scripture says, Ahab's chariot was washed at a pool where the prostitutes bathed. There the dogs licked up his blood—just as Elijah had prophesied. God always has the last word.

There is an irony in God's justice here. At Jezebel's insistence, Ahab had introduced the worship of Baal, along with its cultic prostitution, to the nation of Israel. Now the dogs licked his blood from the pool where the prostitutes regularly bathed. Ahab had shed the blood of Naboth; now his own blood was shed.

God had the last word against Jezebel as well as Ahab. In a few years' time, the Lord anointed Jehu king over Israel and told him to destroy the house of Ahab. Jehu killed all of Ahab's survivors, including Jezebel.

---

2 Kings 9:30–37

Then Jehu went to Jezreel. When Jezebel heard about it, she painted her eyes, arranged her hair and looked out of a window. As Jehu entered the gate, she asked, "Have you come in peace, Zimri, you murderer of your master?"

He looked up at the window and called out, "Who is on my side? Who?" Two or three eunuchs looked down at him. "Throw her down!" Jehu said. So they threw her down, and some of her blood spattered the wall and the horses as they trampled her underfoot.

Jehu went in and ate and drank. "Take care of that cursed woman," he said, "and bury her, for she was a king's daughter." But when they went out to bury her, they found nothing except her skull, her feet and her hands. They went back and told Jehu, who said, "This is the word of the LORD that he spoke through his servant Elijah the Tishbite: On the plot of ground at Jezreel dogs will devour Jezebel's flesh. Jezebel's body will be like refuse on the ground in the plot at Jezreel, so that no one will be able to say, 'This is Jezebel.'"

We do not always see God's justice carried out so swiftly. But we can be assured that He will judge the wicked for causing the innocent to suffer. And His judgment against the unrepentant is not momentary but will last for all of eternity.

Three Types of Judgment

There are three different types of judgment described in Scripture. First, there is an *internal judgment,* which happens when you recognize your own sins and deal with them. Internal judgment is a private matter between you and God.

Second, there is an *external judgment,* which is in God's hands. This is the kind of judgment meted out against Ahab and Jezebel. As I have said, we do not always see God's justice carried out. But third, even when there is no apparent external judgment of sin, we can be sure there will be an *eternal judgment* of sin that will go on forever and ever.

The best judgment of all is internal judgment. When you judge yourself, you literally stop God from judging you externally. "But if we judged ourselves, we would not come under judgment" (1 Cor. 11:31).

Is there something you need to judge in your heart today? Perhaps it is a relationship that does not belong in your life. Perhaps you have possessions or money that should not be yours. Perhaps it is an unbridled greed or covetousness after something or someone. Perhaps it is anger that is eating you up.

Whatever it is, the Holy Spirit is able to tell you what area of your life needs internal judgment. It is the desire of our merciful, loving, compassionate God that we repent of sin the very moment we are convicted of it. You can measure your growth in Christ by how long it takes you to move from conviction to repentance.

If internal judgment does not take place, you will be judged externally. And if that does not bring you to repentance, then you will face eternal judgment. Let the blood of Jesus Christ purify you from every sin.

I am not talking about renewing your commitment or another momentary decision you make under emotional conviction and quickly forget. I am talking about that phone call you need to make. I am talking about that letter you need to write. I am talking about that visit you are dreading but you need to make. I am talking about that restitution you need to pay.

You have the choice whether to place yourself under internal judgment or external judgment or eternal judgment. It's up to you: Will you place yourself under God's mercy or God's judgment?

You must also be careful where you get your advice. For, as we will see next, looking for spiritual guidance in the wrong places can be deadly.

nine

Looking in All the Wrong Places

A t the Synergy Center in Overton, deep in the piney woods of East Texas, you can be reunited with a loved one who has died. One hundred fifty dollars will buy you a session in the center's psychomanteum, a special room constructed for the purpose of contacting the dead.

It works something like this. You walk into the soundproof chamber and take a seat in a comfortable chair, the room's only furniture. You breathe deeply and relax, as instructed by a staff member during your preinterview, in which you talked at length about the departed friend or family member you hope to contact.

Now you open your eyes and look around. The walls, painted black, are almost invisible in the dimly lit room. Your eyes drift to a mirror on the wall in front of you. The chair is offset, so that you can gaze into the mirror without seeing your reflection.

If your visit to the psychomanteum is typical, you will have a paranormal experience. Perhaps the person you are seeking will appear in the mirror, or even come through the glass to stand beside you and converse with you. When you exit the chamber, you will go through a postinterview to evaluate your session. According to the center, clients have reported experiences ranging "from visions, guides and symbols which provided answers to the participant's questions, to out-of-body experiences as well as visits and communication with loved ones who have died."[1]

The use of the psychomanteum to contact the dead dates back to ancient Greece. Elizabeth Hillstrom, associate professor of psychology at Wheaton College, described the Greek custom of consulting oracles in this way:

> *Psychomanteum* is actually another name for the ancient Greek oracles of the dead . . . Those who visited an oracle for this purpose were required to live in very dimly lit underground rooms and passageways for up to a month (probably a very effective way of inducing sensory deprivation). At the end of this time they were led by priests into a large "hall of visions" that was illuminated with

torches. There they gazed into a huge, highly pol-
ished metal caldron (perhaps through water) until
apparitions appeared in its mirrored surfaces.[2]

Dr. Raymond Moody, a psychiatrist who has written about near-death experiences for over twenty years,
has popularized the modern version of the psychomanteum. It is his model that "personal transformation"
centers, such as the Synergy Center, follow.

Since 1990 several hundred of Moody's clients
have entered his psychomanteum, and over half of
them reported encounters with the dead on the first
attempt. Moody recommends the practice as a compo-
nent of grief therapy and as a way to overcome the fear
of death. In December 1993 the psychomanteum made
its debut in popular culture when Oprah Winfrey featured Moody and several of his spirit-seeking clients
on her talk show.

Across America, millions of people are turning to
psychics and channelers and all kinds of occultic powers
for counsel. Even regular churchgoers have become
casual dabblers. According to trends forecaster John
Naisbitt, "What were once considered New Age ideas
are increasingly mainstream. A full two-thirds of
Americans say they have had an ESP experience and
42 percent say they have had 'contact with the dead.'"[3]

Small wonder, then, that it barely raised eyebrows
when the media reported that Nancy Reagan had tried

to control her husband's schedule through consultations with an astrologer, or that Hillary Clinton was having imaginary conversations with Eleanor Roosevelt.

Corporate boardrooms have also become promoters of the occult. American corporations spend $4 billion annually[4] on high-powered consultants who teach employees such New Age doctrines as visualization (to "create your own reality"), meditation (to achieve altered states of consciousness), and even channeling (contacting a spirit guide or your "higher self").

What all of this tells us is that our nation is hungering for spiritual direction but looking for it in all the wrong places. Satan is trying to make the occult respectable in our land. The tragedy is that God does not take this lightly.

Like Father, Like Son

Let's look now at how God dealt with a Hebrew king who turned to the occult for guidance.

After Ahab died, his son Ahaziah became king. About two years later, Ahaziah fell through the latticework in an upper chamber of the palace. (This would be like falling out of a second- or third-story window to the ground below.) The king was seriously injured. So he sent messengers to inquire of Baal-Zebub, the god of Ekron, whether he would recover from this injury or die.

1 Kings 22:51–53; 2 Kings 1:1–17

Ahaziah son of Ahab became king of Israel in Samaria in the seventeenth year of Jehoshaphat king of Judah, and he reigned over Israel two years. He did evil in the eyes of the LORD, because he walked in the ways of his father and mother and in the ways of Jeroboam son of Nebat, who caused Israel to sin. He served and worshiped Baal and provoked the LORD, the God of Israel, to anger, just as his father had done.

After Ahab's death, Moab rebelled against Israel. Now Ahaziah had fallen through the lattice of his upper room in Samaria and injured himself. So he sent messengers, saying to them, "Go and consult Baal-Zebub, the god of Ekron, to see if I will recover from this injury."

But the angel of the LORD said to Elijah the Tishbite, "Go up and meet the messengers of the king of Samaria and ask them, 'Is it because there is no God in Israel that you are going off to consult Baal-Zebub, the god of Ekron?' Therefore this is what the LORD says: 'You will not leave the bed you are lying on. You will certainly die!'" So Elijah went.

When the messengers returned to the king, he asked them, "Why have you come back?"

"A man came to meet us," they replied. "And

he said to us, 'Go back to the king who sent you and tell him, "This is what the LORD says: Is it because there is no God in Israel that you are sending men to consult Baal-Zebub, the god of Ekron? Therefore you will not leave the bed you are lying on. You will certainly die!"'"

The king asked them, "What kind of man was it who came to meet you and told you this?"

They replied, "He was a man with a garment of hair and with a leather belt around his waist."

The king said, "That was Elijah the Tishbite."

Then he sent to Elijah a captain with his company of fifty men. The captain went up to Elijah, who was sitting on the top of a hill, and said to him, "Man of God, the king says, 'Come down!'"

Elijah answered the captain, "If I am a man of God, may fire come down from heaven and consume you and your fifty men!" Then fire fell from heaven and consumed the captain and his men.

At this the king sent to Elijah another captain with his fifty men. The captain said to him, "Man of God, this is what the king says, 'Come down at once!'"

"If I am a man of God," Elijah replied, "may fire come down from heaven and consume you and your fifty men!" Then the fire of God fell from heaven and consumed him and his fifty men.

So the king sent a third captain with his fifty men. This third captain went up and fell on his knees before Elijah. "Man of God," he begged, "please have respect for my life and the lives of these fifty men, your servants! See, fire has fallen from heaven and consumed the first two captains and all their men. But now have respect for my life!"

The angel of the LORD said to Elijah, "Go down with him; do not be afraid of him." So Elijah got up and went down with him to the king.

He told the king, "This is what the LORD says: Is it because there is no God in Israel for you to consult that you have sent messengers to consult Baal-Zebub, the god of Ekron? Because you have done this, you will never leave the bed you are lying on. You will certainly die!" So he died, according to the word of the LORD that Elijah had spoken.

Like father, like son.

Ahab and Jezebel lived a godless lifestyle. So did their children. Ahab compromised his faith and remade Yahweh in the image of Baal, and his son followed suit.

If there is one thing we parents can be sure of, it is that our children are always following our example.

Whether we like it or not, our children are watching what we *do* more than what we *say*. If our children see us put our trust in God, they will grow up putting their trust in God. If our children see us contented and grateful to God for His blessings, they will grow up to be contented and grateful to God. If our children hear us speak the truth all the time, they will grow up always speaking the truth.

But if our children hear us say one thing to a person's face and then hear us slander that person behind his back, our children will become back-stabbers too. If our children see us steal from our employers and cheat on our income taxes, they will grow up to be thieves and frauds. After all, that's the lesson they learned at home.

Let me show how this parent-child model explains one of the puzzling tenets of Scripture. When the Bible talks about generational sin, it is not necessarily talking about something genetic; it is talking about learned behavior. Abraham lied about his wife, Sarah, not once but twice. What did Isaac do? He lied about his wife, Rebekah, in the same fashion. And Abraham's grandson, Jacob, lied to his father in order to steal his brother's inheritance. Lying became a generational sin in that family because children and grandchildren were watching their parents and grandparents, and what the next generation saw the previous generation do was more influential than what they heard them say.

A story is told that after President Lincoln was assassinated, Mrs. Lincoln summoned Mr. Parker, the president's bodyguard, to account for his failure to protect the chief executive.

"Why were you not at the door to keep the assassin out?" she demanded.

With his head bowed, Parker replied, "I have bitterly repented of it, but I did not believe that anyone would try to kill so good a man in such a public place. That belief made me careless. I was attracted by the play and did not see the assassin enter the box."

"You should have seen him. You had no business to be careless." With this Mrs. Lincoln covered her face with her hands, and from deep grief said, "Go now, it is not you I can't forgive; it is the assassin."

Tad, the president's young son, had spent that miserable night beneath his father's desk in the executive office. After this dialogue between his mother and the bodyguard, he was heard to say, "If Pa had lived, he would have forgiven the man who shot him. Pa forgave everybody."

It is obvious that young Lincoln had been watching and listening to his dad. He knew that his dad was a forgiving man, because he had seen that forgiveness demonstrated over and over.

Like it or not, the real legacy we give our children is not money or material possessions. It is not prestige or fame. What we leave our children is the example of our walk with God; that is their godly heritage.

Lord of the Flies

As young Tad Lincoln had seen his father's example of forgiveness, Ahaziah had witnessed his father's compromise of his faith.

I cannot help but think that perhaps Ahaziah saw his daddy celebrating all of the Jewish holidays in public while he trusted Baal in the privacy of his palace. Ahaziah saw his father pay lip service to his Jewish heritage, but privately he talked more about Baal than Yahweh. Ahaziah observed how King Ahab had his own brand of religion, his own idea of God, his own morality and ethics. And so he followed in his father's footsteps.

When Ahaziah got into trouble, what did he do? Did he go to Yahweh and ask for help? No. Did he say, "Let me find out if there is a prophet of God here to pray for me"? No. When he got into trouble, Ahaziah turned to a pagan god, Baal-Zebub. He turned to the occult for revelation about the future.

After the king was injured, he wanted to know whether he was going to live or die. The first thing he thought about was what he had learned from his daddy, who had always taken his wife's gods and goddesses very seriously. So Ahaziah sent messengers to Ekron, where they worshiped a god whose name was Baal-Zebub, a god known locally as the god of the future. Instead of coming in repentance and asking God to heal and forgive him, Ahaziah went to inquire of Baal-Zebub.

Look with me for a moment to see what Baal-Zebub is all about. He is mentioned in the Old Testament four times, all in this first chapter of 2 Kings. Baal-Zebub is a strange and eerie sounding name, but he was considered to be a very powerful god.

The name Baal means "god" or "lord." In the Hebrew language, *zebub* refers to a fly. In fact, the word is the same in Arabic and Aramaic. In its very ugliness, the name Baal-Zebub means "god of the flies." Ekron, one of the five major cities of Philistia, was the center of worship of Baal-Zebub, this lord of the flies.

Flies have often plagued the Middle Eastern people. These plagues are like what you would see in a horror movie, where millions of flies swarm the homes and streets and farms of a community. There were no insect repellents back then, so when a plague of flies struck, the people were terrified. They believed that Baal-Zebub sent these plagues, so in order to appease him and beseech him to remove the flies, they would bow down and worship this false god.

Baal-Zebub was also like a storefront fortune-teller, dispensing advice about future events. If you wanted to know the future of your job situation, or whether there was romance ahead, or if you would come into some money, what did you do? You would call the 900 number and ask the priest or the priestess of Baal-Zebub to tell you all about it. And fifty or a hundred dollars later you would have some information that was probably 80 percent inaccurate. But that wouldn't matter. You would feel real good—at least until your telephone bill arrived.

There were no telephone psychics in biblical times, of course, but the way people consulted Baal-Zebub was very similar to the way some people regularly call the psychic hot lines promoted on late-night television.

Those people may tell you, "But it's really just a harmless bit of fun." And it's true that in the fine print at the bottom of each television ad for a psychic network is this advisory: "For entertainment only." In other words, "Please don't rely on our advice. We're just having some fun (and making a lot of money at your expense) and want you to have fun too."

Besides being a waste of money, consulting a telephone psychic—or inquiring of Baal-Zebub—is not just harmless fun. Let's look at a New Testament passage that gives more information about who Baal-Zebub is.

Matthew 12:22–28
Then they brought him a demon-possessed man

who was blind and mute, and Jesus healed him, so that he could both talk and see. All the people were astonished and said, "Could this be the Son of David?"

But when the Pharisees heard this, they said, "It is only by Beelzebub, the prince of demons, that this fellow drives out demons."

Jesus knew their thoughts and said to them, "Every kingdom divided against itself will be ruined, and every city or household divided against itself will not stand. If Satan drives out Satan, he is divided against himself. How then can his kingdom stand? And if I drive out demons by Beelzebub, by whom do your people drive them out? So then, they will be your judges. But if I drive out demons by the Spirit of God, then the kingdom of God has come upon you."

Matthew 12 says that Jesus healed a blind, mute, demon-possessed man. No longer the sightless, speechless prisoner of a demon, the man could both talk and see after Jesus marvelously released him from his bondage.

Every faithful Jew knew that when the Messiah came, the mark of His messiahship would be the release of people from the power of Satan. The people were absolutely ecstatic over what they saw, and they were asking, "Could this be the long-awaited Messiah? Could this be the Son of David?"

But look at the predictable reaction of the self-righteous Pharisees. "It is only by Beelzebub, the prince of demons, that this fellow drives out demons" (Matt. 12:24). (The variation in the spelling of the name here simply reflects the difference between the original Greek and Hebrew words. Baal-Zebub and Beelzebub are one and the same.)

The Pharisees accused Jesus of casting out demons by the power of Baal-Zebub, "the prince of demons"—which is another name for Satan. Jesus rebuked their unbelief and told them that Satan does not cast out Satan. The point is this: Our Lord acknowledged the reality of that sinister demonic force, Baal-Zebub, the prince of demons.

So for Ahaziah to inquire of Baal-Zebub whether he would recover from his injury was the same as asking Satan himself. And when you are tempted to look up your horoscope, or to call the psychic hot line, or to consult with channelers or fortune-tellers, or to use a Ouija board or tarot cards for guidance about the future, you are dealing with the storefront of Baal-Zebub. You are dealing with Satan himself. And you will expose yourself to dangers that you cannot even imagine.

This is not a bit of harmless fun. This is playing with fire. You are tempting God and opening yourself up to satanic powers.

The Price for Consulting Baal-Zebub

How did God respond to Ahaziah's reliance on Baal-Zebub? His response demonstrates just how seriously God takes it when His people dabble in the occult.

God told Elijah to meet the messengers Ahaziah had sent to Baal-Zebub. Elijah obeyed God and told the king's men to go back and ask him, "Is it because there is no God in Israel that you are going off to consult Baal-Zebub, the god of Ekron?" (2 Kings 1:3).

It had been about ten years since the confrontation with Ahab over the murder of Naboth. Elijah was now ready to confront a second generation of godless leadership in Israel. So Elijah told the messengers on their way to Ekron exactly what the Lord had told him to say. "Tell Ahaziah," Elijah warned them, "that because he has not sought the Lord, he will not leave the bed he is lying on. He will certainly die!"

The messengers went back to King Ahaziah and delivered the bad news. Imagine their wild tale about a strange prophet who had stopped them to give this dire message. Ahaziah asked the messengers to describe the man. When they did, Ahaziah knew it was Elijah. He remembered how Elijah was a pain in his father's side, and now the old prophet had become a pain in his side too.

Have you ever noticed that when you live a godly life in the midst of unbelieving family members or business associates or neighbors, you can become a pain to them? Don't go out of your way to become one, because you already are by the very nature of your godly life. You are both an intrigue and an irritation to them, an enigma and a rebuke.

And eventually they will have to react in one of two ways. Either they will turn to God or they will become very, very angry. That is what happened here with Ahaziah. Elijah's message and rebuke could have caused him to repent, but it didn't. Instead, Ahaziah became enraged, and he rejected God altogether.

This king, like his father, did not repent at the word of the living God. Instead, he chose bitterness and anger toward the man of God. So he sent a captain and fifty men to go and bring Elijah back, probably intending to throw the prophet in jail or to kill him, as his mother had once vowed to do.

The captain was disrespectful to Elijah. He spoke in a contemptuous way to the great prophet of the nation. So Elijah said, "If I am a man of God, may fire come down from heaven and consume you and your fifty men" (2 Kings 1:10). And zap! Fire came down and consumed them.

Did the king repent after that dramatic but disastrous attempt to get Elijah? No. He sent another fifty of his cronies. This captain did the same thing, and the same thing happened to them.

Stubborn and defiant, Ahaziah sent yet a third group. But the captain of this company had wised up. He must have been thinking, *Even if the king is a fool, I am not going to be one.* So he spoke in humility to Elijah, asking the prophet to please come with him, out of respect for his life and the lives of his men.

In response to the man's humility, the Lord instructed Elijah to go with him to the palace. Elijah was no longer afraid as he had been when Jezebel had threatened to take his life. Why was he not afraid? Because this time he had waited on a word from the Lord. He was going in obedience to God. So he marched right into the bedroom of King Ahaziah, looked him straight in the eye, and delivered the message himself: "Is it because there is no God in Israel for you to consult that you have sent messengers to consult Baal-Zebub, the god of Ekron? Because you have done this, you will never leave the bed you are lying on. You will certainly die!" (2 Kings 1:16).

The king still was not repentant, and he died in accordance with this word from God.

Be Careful Where You Get Your Advice

Ahaziah's desire to shop at the spiritual storefront of Baal-Zebub, the prince of demons, cost him his life. Because he turned to the occult rather than to God, he received a death sentence.

Hebrews 13:8 says that God is the same yesterday, today, and forever. And the way we see God working in Scripture should teach us what pleases Him and what does not please Him, what honors Him and what dishonors Him.

It may seem that God's judgment against Ahaziah's sin was swift and severe. But what happened to the wicked king was actually the fulfillment of God's warning given hundreds of years earlier. The judgment of God is never arbitrary. God's judgment culminates only after a whole lot of forewarning. And those who heed God's warning and repent will not come under His judgment.

"Do not turn to mediums or seek out spiritists," God had cautioned His people centuries earlier, "for you will be defiled by them" (Lev. 19:31). He also said, "I will set my face against the person who turns to mediums and spiritists to prostitute himself by following them, and I will cut him off from his people" (Lev. 20:6). Mediums and spiritists are among the things the Bible says are "detestable to the LORD" (Deut. 18:11–12), and people who engaged in these practices were to be put to death (Lev. 20:27).

Be careful where you get your advice!

Those who would follow Dr. Raymond Moody into his modern psychomanteum would do well to heed the advice of Isaiah: "When men tell you to consult mediums and spiritists, who whisper and mutter, should not a people inquire of their God? Why consult the dead on behalf of the living?" (8:19).

The church of Jesus Christ must not go looking for spiritual guidance in all the wrong places. We must get our guidance from the Word of God and the leading of the Holy Spirit—whose direction, I must point out, will never contradict Scripture.

Let's look now at a biblical heroine who was careful where she got her advice. She followed the counsel of a godly man—and saved all the Jews living in Persia.

ten

For Such a Time as This

*C*orrie ten Boom often marveled at her sister Betsie's ability to accept Ravensbruck as God's sovereign will for their lives. The two spoke frequently of the kind of ministry they would have after the war. Betsie dreamed about renovating one of Hitler's concentration camps and operating it as an outreach to those who had been so scarred emotionally by the horrors of war. Corrie was astonished when she realized that Betsie was not talking about a ministry to their fellow prisoners. Instead, Betsie intended to mend the souls of their German torturers!

"Corrie, if people can be taught to hate, they can be taught to love!" . . .

She went on, almost forgetting in her excitement to keep her voice to a whisper, while I slowly took in the fact that she was talking about our guards. I glanced at the matron seated at the desk ahead of us. I saw a gray uniform and a visored hat; Betsie saw a wounded human being.

And I wondered, not for the first time, what sort of a person she was, this sister of mine . . . what kind of road she followed while I trudged beside her on the all-too-solid earth.[1]

Even though Corrie struggled with forgiving those who held her captive, she eventually did accept the fact that God had sent them to Ravensbruck for a purpose. She began to view her imprisonment from an eternal perspective.

When you are dying—when you stand at the gate of eternity—you see things from a different perspective than when you think you may live for a long time. I had been standing at that gate for many months, living in Barracks 28 in the shadow of the crematorium. Every time I saw the smoke pouring from the hideous smokestacks I knew it was the last remains of some poor woman who had been with me in Ravensbruck. Often I asked myself, "When will it be my time to be killed or die?"

But I was not afraid. Following Betsie's death, God's Presence was even more real . . .

One week before the order came to kill all the women of my age, I was free. I still do not understand all the details of my release from Ravensbruck. All I know is, it was a miracle of God.[2]

On the day Corrie was to be released, she was standing in the prison yard awaiting final orders when another prisoner whispered to her that two of their friends had died that morning.

Tiny! "Oh, Lord, thank You for letting me point her to Jesus who has now ushered her safely into Your Presence." And Marie. I knew her well. She lived in my barracks and had attended my Bible talks. Like Tiny, Marie had also accepted Jesus as her Lord. I looked back at the long row of barracks. "Lord, if it was only for Tiny and Marie— that they might come to know you before they died—then it was all worthwhile!"[3]

Corrie never understood, humanly speaking, why the Germans released her just one week before she was scheduled to die in the crematorium. But from a spiritual standpoint it was obvious: Ultimately, the Nazis were not the final authority over the inmates of Ravensbruck; God was.

Gaining an Eternal Perspective

Like so many other believers who have endured great suffering, the ten Boom sisters drew strength from their understanding of the sovereignty of God. They knew that He had allowed their suffering for His divine purposes. Ravensbruck was not an accident; it was part of God's plan for their lives. Corrie learned to step back and see things from an eternal perspective, to see the "big picture" of His sovereign plan for the universe. If only for two souls, she concluded, her suffering was all worthwhile.

Gaining an eternal perspective on our circumstances is not always easy, and it is not something that is achieved overnight. It comes from placing ourselves in God's will every day of our lives and trusting Him to keep us, no matter what happens. To me that's one of the most frustrating aspects of understanding God's plans and purposes. I often wish God would fax me a road map, with all the destinations highlighted and all the travel details spelled out in advance.

Yet it is the mercy of God that He does not unfold His eternal purposes for us all at once. Think of Corrie ten Boom. If she had known in advance that her entire family would be arrested, that her father would die in prison, that she and Betsie would be sent to a concentration camp where they would suffer unfathomable deprivation, that Betsie would die there—how could she have coped with that knowledge?

Like so many biblical heroines, Corrie was an ordinary woman called to do something extraordinary at a moment of crisis. She was a simple watchmaker from Haarlem—a woman with many faults and shortcomings, but a woman who loved God and treasured His Word. When the moment of crisis arrived, her passion for the Bible and the people through whom it came— the Jewish people—led her to risk her life. The ten Boom family saved many Jews in Holland by hiding them in a secret room in their home. Through the Bible Corrie miraculously smuggled into a German concentration camp, many souls heard the gospel and gained eternal life—just moments before they lost their lives, in some cases.

That was God's purpose for Corrie's life, and in retrospect she could plainly see it and rejoice in it. But before that moment of crisis came, she had no inkling that she had come into the kingdom of God "for such a time as this."

Let's look now at a biblical heroine who faced her own moment of crisis and, through her obedience to God's will for her life, saved all of her people.

A Jewish Queen for Persia

We know this biblical heroine as Esther, although her Hebrew name was Hadassah. Like the other Jews exiled to Persia, however, she was forced to take a foreign name. After her parents died one of Esther's relatives, Mordecai, raised her as his own daughter. This godly man became a high-ranking official in the Persian kingdom.

When King Xerxes deposed the queen, court officials proposed a sort of beauty pageant to find a new wife for him. From each province commissioners selected the most beautiful young woman, then they brought the group of women to the royal harem. Esther, who had kept her Jewish identity secret at Mordecai's instruction, won the king's favor.

And that's how a Jewish beauty became the queen of Persia.

The biblical account of Esther centers around the plot of a wicked man, Haman, who had vowed to destroy not only Mordecai but all of the Jews living in Xerxes' kingdom. Haman lied to the king and tricked him into issuing an edict that called for the elimination of all the Jewish people, "young and old, women and little children—on a single day" (Est. 3:13). We know from other sources that the date Haman selected was March 7, 473 B.C., about eleven months after the edict was issued.

When Mordecai learned of this genocidal edict, he went into mourning. He began to fast and pray. Because he could not enter the royal palace in sackcloth and ashes, Mordecai sent a messenger to Queen Esther, asking her to intervene with the king on behalf of her people.

Esther 4:1–16

When Mordecai learned of all that had been done, he tore his clothes, put on sackcloth and ashes, and went out into the city, wailing loudly and bitterly. But he went only as far as the king's gate, because no one clothed in sackcloth was allowed to enter it. In every province to which the edict and order of the king came, there was great mourning among the Jews, with fasting, weeping and wailing. Many lay in sackcloth and ashes.

When Esther's maids and eunuchs came and told her about Mordecai, she was in great distress. She sent clothes for him to put on instead of his sackcloth, but he would not accept them. Then Esther summoned Hathach, one of the king's eunuchs assigned to attend her, and ordered him to find out what was troubling Mordecai and why.

So Hathach went out to Mordecai in the open square of the city in front of the king's gate. Mordecai told him everything that had happened to him, including the exact amount of money Haman had promised to pay into the royal treasury for the destruction of the Jews. He also gave him a copy of the text of the edict for their annihilation, which had been published in Susa, to show to Esther and explain it to her, and he told him to urge her to go into the king's presence to beg for mercy and plead with him for her people.

Hathach went back and reported to Esther what Mordecai had said. Then she instructed him to say to Mordecai, "All the king's officials and the people of the royal provinces know that for any man or woman who approaches the king in the inner court without being summoned the king has but one law: that he be put to death. The only exception to this is for the king to extend the gold scepter to him and spare his life. But thirty days have passed since I was called to go to the king."

When Esther's words were reported to Mordecai, he sent back this answer: "Do not think that because you are in the king's house you alone of all the Jews will escape. For if you remain silent at this time, relief and deliverance for the Jews will arise from another place, but you and your father's family will perish. And who knows but that you have come to royal position for such a time as this?"

Then Esther sent this reply to Mordecai: "Go, gather together all the Jews who are in Susa, and fast for me. Do not eat or drink for three days, night or day. I and my maids will fast as you do. When this is done, I will go to the king, even though it is against the law. And if I perish, I perish."

In her reply Esther reminded Mordecai that, by royal decree, she could not enter the king's presence uninvited—in fact, no one could. Historical records testify that this was indeed a Persian law. The penalty for violating it was death, unless the king immediately pardoned the offender by extending his gold scepter. "The king has not sent for me in thirty days," Esther told Mordecai. "If I go before him to beg for mercy, it could cost me my life."

We see from the biblical text that Mordecai understood how God's sovereign purposes are fulfilled. He warned Esther that her position as queen would not automatically protect her from being slaughtered. Then he said, "If you don't intevene, deliverance will come from another source." Mordecai knew that God would not allow His chosen people to be completely wiped out, for from their lineage would come the promised Messiah. That was God's eternal plan, declared through His prophets. Nevertheless, Mordecai wanted to spare as many as possible from wanton destruction.

Then Mordecai issued a challenge to Esther: "What if the very reason you have been elevated to the royal court is to be the instrument God uses to save your people? Think about it. How did you, a Jewish woman, become the wife of the king of Persia? Why are you now in such a place of prominence and influence?"

Esther faced a moment of crisis. She had to make a

choice. She could rise to her destiny and risk her life to spare her people. Or she could refuse to fulfill God's purpose for her life, and He would send deliverance through someone else. But she would pay a price for rejecting God's plan, and would quite possibly lose her life anyway.

As Mordecai fasted and prayed about the situation, he began to see clearly how Esther fit into God's sovereign plan for His people. A unique opportunity had presented itself to Esther, and Mordecai understood that it was God who had arranged for her to be in this position for this very moment. God had brought her into the Persian kingdom "for such a time as this."

"If I Perish, I Perish"

A similar challenge could be addressed to every one of us today: "What if you have been born into the kingdom of God for such a time as this?" You will either accomplish God's plan for your life, or you will reject it to your own peril. You can go to the king in faith, or you can remain paralyzed by fear. You will either seize the opportunity or lament its loss forever.

Esther met the challenge. She told Mordecai, "Tell all the Jews in Susa to fast for three days, and I will call my attendants to join with me in fasting for three days. Then I will go into the presence of the king, even though it is against the law . . . And if I perish, I perish."

What a magnificent commitment to God's plan. Esther made that commmitment fully aware of the potential cost. "If I perish, I perish," she said, picturing in her mind the possibility that the king would not pardon her violation of the law and that she would be seized by the royal guards and executed.

I won't take time to relate the rest of the story to you, but the bottom line is that Esther did not perish. The king extended the scepter to her and spared her life. Then he issued a new edict permitting the Jews to defend themselves, and the Persians became afraid of killing them. I encourage you to read the entire book of Esther and see how God used her when she was completely committed to fulfilling God's purpose for her life.

Daniel made a similar commitment when he continued to pray to God in spite of a king's edict. He knew he could be thrown to the lions for breaking the law, but Daniel was obedient to God. He went into the lions' den thinking, *If I perish, I perish*. The king and everyone else in the kingdom soon learned that Daniel served a God who was in control of the lions. He supernaturally shut their mouths, and Daniel walked out without a scratch (Dan. 6).

How could Job say of God, "Though he slay me, yet will I hope in him" (Job 13:15)? Job did not understand why so many calamities struck him at one time, yet he still trusted God. If anybody was ever entitled to say, "If

God is in control, why is my life such a mess?" it was Job. Yet he held to his faith, and in time God proved that He was indeed in control of Job's circumstances and that there had been a purpose for his suffering.

Another biblical hero whose circumstances in life could often be described as a mess was the apostle Paul. Listen to this catalog of his trials from Scripture:

> Five times I received from the Jews the forty lashes minus one. Three times I was beaten with rods, once I was stoned, three times I was shipwrecked, I spent a night and a day in the open sea, I have been constantly on the move. I have been in danger from rivers, in danger from bandits, in danger from my own countrymen, in danger from Gentiles; in danger in the city, in danger in the country, in danger at sea; and in danger from false brothers. I have labored and toiled and have often gone without sleep; I have known hunger and thirst and have often gone without food; I have been cold and naked. Besides everything else, I face daily the pressure of my concern for all the churches. (2 Cor. 11:24–28)

Yet Paul referred to all these things as "light and momentary troubles" (2 Cor. 4:17). He said, "We are hard pressed on every side, but not crushed; perplexed, but not in despair; persecuted, but not abandoned; struck down, but not destroyed" (2 Cor. 4:8–9).

How could he be so optimistic in the face of such crushing circumstances as beatings, stoning, shipwrecks, and hunger? Because Paul recognized that God was in control, he could say confidently, "We may be down, but we're not out. The circumstances are pressing, but we will not be crushed by them." Paul knew he was fulfilling God's purpose for his life, and therefore God would protect him and sustain him through every trial, even to the point of death. He wrote to Timothy that he was not ashamed to be suffering for the sake of the gospel, "because I know whom I have believed, and am convinced that he is able to guard what I have entrusted to him for that day" (2 Tim. 1:12).

Paul also understood that the Roman government could not kill him unless their death sentence against him had first passed through God's hand. When that moment arrived, he was prepared for it. Some of Paul's last recorded words were these: "I have fought the good fight, I have finished the race, I have kept the faith. Now there is in store for me the crown of righteousness" (2 Tim. 4:7–8).

Like Esther, like Daniel, like Job, like Paul, you must let faith take you to the point where you can say, "If I perish, I perish." Or, "If I suffer, I suffer." For in all likelihood, following God's purpose for you will not cost you your life—at least not in America. Here in this country we enjoy so much freedom and so much prosperity that we do not appreciate the fact that most of the Christians in the world are persecuted for their faith. We get so caught up in the ingrained notion that we are guaranteed "the pursuit of happiness" that we are surprised, and sometimes easily defeated, when we encounter trials and difficulties.

If your life is a mess right now, ask God to show you why. It may be that you are suffering through the consequences of past sins or mistakes you have made. Even though God forgives us instantly, He does not automatically cancel the repercussions of our actions. He may allow you to endure difficulty you have brought upon yourself, but He will see you through it if you let Him be in control of the situation and ask Him to show you His purpose for your life. He can and will work out every situation for your good, even when you have failed miserably. Turn to God in repentance, and trust in His love, mercy, and faithfulness to His children.

Or it could be that you are in great difficulty precisely because you *are* following God's plan for your life. In that case, rejoice in the Lord! Remember what we have learned from the life of Elijah: that God has a hiding place for you, a place of provision, protection, and preparation; that God can take your meager resources and multiply them miraculously; that God is working on both ends of your situation at once; that the blasting of a storm often occurs in the midst of a blessing; that God wants you to quit wobbling and take a stand for the gospel of Christ; that God is faithful to all His promises; that God has compassion for His servants who are battling discouragement or depression; and that God will always have the last word.

And, above all, remember this: Our sovereign Lord is in control.

Notes

Chapter 1
Is God Really in Control?

1. See Jeremiah 1:5.
2. See Matthew 10:30.
3. While Lebanon at the time had a Christian majority, almost as many Muslims lived there; it was a popular place for citizens of Arab countries to visit.

Chapter 2
Hidden for God's Purposes

1. Nancy M. Reichardt, "Soap Log," United Feature Syndicate, 25 January 1998.

Chapter 3
Faith That Risks Everything

1. Genesis 41:56—42:2.
2. Joshua 2.
3. Acts 8:26–40.

Chapter 5
Stop Wobbling and Take a Stand

1. Acts 10.
2. Acts 23:23—25:27.
3. Mike Wallace reporting, "Sexuality 101," *60 Minutes,* CBS News, 22 March 1998.
4. Robert H. Knight, "The National Endowment: It's Time to Free the Arts," a policy paper published in 1995 by the Family Research Council urging the 104th Congress to "zero-budget" the NEA.
5. Don Feder, "The NEA's Latest Bloody Atrocity," *Boston Herald,* 21 July 1994, distributed by Creators Syndicate, Inc.
6. Stephanie Cash, "Ron Athey at P.S. 122" (New York, New York; Review of Exhibitions), *Art in America,* Feb. 1995 (vol. 83, no. 2), 99.
7. "I am the gate; whoever enters through me will be saved" (John 10:9). "I am the way and the truth and the life. No one comes to the Father except through me" (John 14:6).

8. "I know your deeds, that you are neither cold nor hot. I wish you were either one or the other! So, because you are lukewarm—neither hot nor cold—I am about to spit [vomit] you out of my mouth" (Rev. 3:15–16).

9. James 1:8.

10. "Always be prepared to give an answer to everyone who asks you to give the reason for the hope that you have" (1 Peter 3:15).

11. "By this all men will know that you are my disciples, if you love one another" (John 13:35).

Chapter 7
Dealing with Depression and Discouragement

1. The account of the Surrey Music Hall catastrophe and its effects on Charles Spurgeon is taken from the following sources: "Our First Seven Years," *The Sword and the Trowel,* April 1876 (available online through The Spurgeon Archives, www.spurgeon.org); John Piper, "Charles Spurgeon: Preaching Through Adversity," *The Founders Journal,* Issue 23 (Winter 1996); and Charles H. Spurgeon, Lecture XI: "The Minister's Fainting Fits," *Lectures to My Students* (Pasadena, TX: Pilgrim Publications, 1995).

2. Spurgeon, *Lectures,* 176.

3. Ibid., 177.

4. Charles Spurgeon, "The Christian's Heaviness and Rejoicing," sermon delivered at the Music Hall, Royal

Survey Gardens, November 7, 1858 (available online through The Spurgeon Archives, www.spurgeon.org).

5. Ibid.

6. Charles Spurgeon, "Our Compassionate High Priest," sermon delivered at Metropolitan Tabernacle, April 3, 1890, reprinted in AGES Digital Library, C. H. Spurgeon Collection, Vol. 4, 63.

7. "The Good News About Depression," 1998, NetHealth, a division of Epicenter Communications, Inc. (available online at www.depression.com).

8. Ibid.

9. Spurgeon, *Lectures,* 167, 169.

Chapter 8
When the Innocent Suffer

1. "Profiles of the Austin-area victims of Tuesday's storms," *Austin American-Statesman,* 1 June 1997.

2. Darrel W. Amundsen, "The Anguish and Agonies of Charles Spurgeon," *Christian History,* Issue 29 (Vol. X, No. 1), 1991, 25.

3. Corrie ten Boom with John and Elizabeth Sherrill, *The Hiding Place* (Washington Depot, Conn.: Chosen Books, 1971), 197.

4. Nina Shea, *In the Lion's Den* (Nashville: Broadman and Holman, 1997), 36–37.

Chapter 9
Looking in All the Wrong Places

1. From the home page of the Synergy Center.
2. Elizabeth L. Hillstrom, *Testing the Spirits* (Downers Grove, IL: InterVarsity Press, 1995), 184.
3. John Naisbitt and Patricia Aburdene, *Megatrends 2000* (New York: William Morrow and Company, Inc., 1990), 293.
4. Ibid., 294.

Chapter 10
For Such a Time as This

1. *Hiding Place,* 161.
2. Corrie ten Boom with Jamie Buckingham, *Tramp for the Lord* (New York: Jove Publications, Inc., 1985) (originally published by Fleming H. Revell, Old Tappan, NJ, 1974), 21.
3. *Tramp for the Lord,* 22.

About the
Author

Michael Youssef, Ph.D., was born in the Middle East and is the founding pastor of The Church of The Apostles, an evangelical church in Atlanta, Georgia. He completed his theological training in Australia and received his master's degree from Fuller Seminary and his doctorate from Emory University. He is internationally known as a trainer of evangelical leaders, having consulted with and served as the managing director of the Haggai Institute for Advanced Leadership Training.

He is the president and host teacher of the national radio ministry, *Leading the Way with Dr. Michael Youssef*, where he is heard on hundreds of stations around the world. His previous books include *The Leadership Style of Jesus; America, Oil, and the Islamic Mind;* and *Know Your Real Enemy.*

LOOK FOR THIS OTHER BOOK BY MICHAEL YOUSSEF

Know Your Real Enemy

Dr. Youssef provides readers with a detailed plan for identifying and defeating the real enemy of Christians. But the real enemy is not the nitpicking spouse, the overbearing boss, or complainers in the church. The real enemy is Satan. In this inspirational study, Youssef exposes Satan for who he really is — a deceiver out to destroy you — and shows believers that they are winners in the eyes of the Lord.

0-7852-7102-3 • Hardcover • 224 pages